The writings of Origen Vol. II, Book V

by

Origen

The writings of Origen Vol. II, Book V
by Origen

ISBN: 978-93-59326-32-0

Published by

DOUBLE 9 BOOKS

2/13-B, Ansari Road
Daryaganj, New Delhi – 110002
info@double9books.com
www.double9books.com
Tel. 011-40042856

ABOUT THE AUTHOR

Origen (185-254 AD) is regarded as a pivotal figure in the formation of Christian philosophy. He was a prominent early Christian philosopher and theologian. He was born in Alexandria, Egypt, and spent the majority of his life there, where he lectured and published extensively on a number of themes including theology, philosophy, and biblical exegesis. Origen's work is distinguished by deep intellectual curiosity and a commitment to investigating the more profound aspects of Christian doctrine. He was known for his intensive scholarship and willingness to debating a wide range of philosophical and religious topics in his pursuit of truth. Origen made substantial contributions to Christian thought, yet his legacy has been controversial. Because his work was generally considered as being excessively speculative and susceptible to non-Christian conceptions, Church authorities finally deemed some of his ideas heretical.

CONTENTS

BOOK V

Chapter I

It is not, my reverend Ambrosius, because we seek after many words—a thing which is forbidden, and in the indulgence of which it is impossible to avoid sin [842] —that we now begin the fifth book of our reply to the treatise of Celsus, but with the endeavour, so far as may be within our power, to leave none of his statements without examination, and especially those in which it might appear to some that he had skilfully assailed us and the Jews. If it were possible, indeed, for me to enter along with my words into the conscience of every one without exception who peruses this work, and to extract each dart which wounds him who is not completely protected with the "whole armour" of God, and apply a rational medicine to cure the wound inflicted by Celsus, which prevents those who listen to his words from remaining "sound in the faith," I would do so. But since it is the work of God alone, in conformity with His own Spirit, and along with that of Christ, to take up His abode invisibly in those persons whom He judges worthy of being visited; so, on the other hand, is *our* object to try, by means of arguments and treatises, to confirm men in their faith, and to earn the name of "workmen needing not to be ashamed, rightly dividing the word of truth." [843] And there is one thing above all which it appears to us we ought to do, if we would discharge faithfully the task enjoined upon us by you, and that is to overturn to the best of our ability the confident assertions of Celsus. Let us then quote such assertions of his as follow those which we have already refuted (the reader must decide whether we have done so successfully or not), and let us reply to them. And may God grant that we approach not our subject with our understanding and reason empty and devoid of divine inspiration, that the faith of those whom we wish to aid may not depend upon human wisdom, but that, receiving the "mind" of Christ from His Father, who alone can bestow it, and being strengthened by participating in the word of God, we may pull down "every high thing that exalteth itself against the knowledge of God," [844] and the imagination of Celsus, who exalts himself against us, and against Jesus, and also against Moses and the prophets, in order that He who "gave the word to those who published it with great power" [845] may supply us also, and bestow upon us "great power," so that faith in the word and power of God may be implanted in the minds of all who will peruse our work.

Chapter II

We have now, then, to refute that statement of his which runs as follows: "O Jews and Christians, no God or son of a God either came or will come down [to earth]. But if you mean that certain angels did so, then what do you call them? Are they gods, or some other race of beings? Some other race of beings [doubtless], and in all probability demons." Now as Celsus here is guilty of repeating himself (for in the preceding pages such assertions have been frequently advanced by him), it is unnecessary to discuss the matter at greater length, seeing what we have already said upon this point may suffice. We shall mention, however, a few considerations out of a greater number, such as we deem in harmony with our former arguments, but which have not altogether the same bearing as they, and by which we shall show that in asserting generally that no God, or son of God, ever descended [among men], he overturns not only the opinions entertained by the majority of mankind regarding the manifestation of Deity, but also what was formerly admitted by himself. For if the general statement, that "no God or son of God has come down or will come down," be truly maintained by Celsus, it is manifest that we have here overthrown the belief in the existence of gods upon the earth who had descended from heaven either to predict the future to mankind or to heal them by means of divine responses; and neither the Pythian Apollo, nor Esculapius, nor any other among those supposed to have done so, would be a god descended from heaven. He might, indeed, either be a god who had obtained as his lot [the obligation] to dwell on earth for ever, and be thus a fugitive, as it were, from the abode of the gods, or he might be one who had no power to share in the society of the gods in heaven; [846] or else Apollo, and Esculapius, and those others who are believed to perform acts on earth, would not be gods, but only certain demons, much inferior to those wise men among mankind, who on account of their virtue ascend to the vault [847] of heaven.

Chapter III

But observe how, in his desire to subvert our opinions, he who never acknowledged himself throughout his whole treatise to be an Epicurean, is convicted of being a deserter to that sect. And now is the time for you, [reader], who peruse the works of Celsus, and give your assent to what has been advanced, either to overturn the belief in a God who visits the human race, and exercises a providence over each individual man, or to grant this, and prove the falsity of the assertions of Celsus. If you, then, wholly annihilate providence, you will falsify those assertions of his in which he grants the existence of "God and a providence," in order that you may maintain the truth of your own position; but if, on the other hand, you still admit the existence of providence, because you do not assent to the dictum of Celsus, that "neither has a God nor the son of a God come down nor is to come down [848] to mankind," why not rather carefully ascertain from the statements made regarding Jesus, and the prophecies uttered concerning Him, who it is that we are to consider as having come down to the human race as God, and the Son of God?—whether that Jesus who said and ministered so much, or those who, under pretence of oracles and divinations, do not reform the morals of their worshippers, but who have besides apostatized from the pure and holy worship and honour due to the Maker of all things, and who tear away the souls of those who give heed to them from the one only visible and true God, under a pretence of paying honour to a multitude of deities?

Chapter IV

But since he says, in the next place, as if the Jews or Christians had answered regarding those who come down to visit the human race, that they were angels: "But if ye say that they are angels, what do you call them?" he continues, "Are they gods, or some other race of beings?" and then again introduces us as if answering, "Some other race of beings, and probably demons," —let us proceed to notice these remarks. For we indeed acknowledge that angels are "ministering spirits," and we say that "they are sent forth to minister for them who shall be heirs of salvation;" [849] and that they ascend, bearing the supplications of men, to the purest of the heavenly places in the universe, or even to supercelestial regions purer still; [850] and that they come down from these, conveying to each one, according to his deserts, something enjoined by God to be conferred by them upon those who are to be the recipients of His benefits. Having thus learned to call these beings "angels" from their employments, we find that because they are divine they are sometimes termed "God" in the sacred Scriptures, [851] but not so that we are commanded to honour and worship in place of God those who minister to us, and bear to us His blessings. For every prayer, and supplication, and intercession, and thanksgiving, is to be sent up to the Supreme God through the High Priest, who is above all the angels, the living Word and God. And to the Word Himself shall we also pray and make intercessions, and offer thanksgivings and supplications to Him, if we have the capacity of distinguishing between the proper use and abuse of prayer. [852]

Chapter V

For to invoke angels without having obtained a knowledge of their nature greater than is possessed by men, would be contrary to reason. But, conformably to our hypothesis, let this knowledge of them, which is something wonderful and mysterious, be obtained. Then this knowledge, making known to us their nature, and the offices to which they are severally appointed, will not permit us to pray with confidence to any other than to the Supreme God, who is sufficient for all things, and that through our Saviour the Son of God, who is the Word, and Wisdom, and Truth, and everything else which the writings of God's prophets and the apostles of Jesus entitle Him. And it is enough to secure that the holy angels of God be propitious to us, and that they do all things on our behalf, that our disposition of mind towards God should imitate as far as it is within the power of human nature the example of these holy angels, who again follow the example of their God; and that the conceptions which we entertain of His Son, the Word, so far as attainable by us, should not be opposed to the clearer conceptions of Him which the holy angels possess, but should daily approach these in clearness and distinctness. But because Celsus has not read our Holy Scriptures, he gives himself an answer as if it came from us, saying that we "assert that the angels who come down from heaven to confer benefits on mankind are a different race from the gods," and adds that "in all probability they would be called demons by us:" not observing that the name "demons" is not a term of indifferent meaning like that of "men," among whom some are good and some bad, nor yet a term of excellence like that of "the gods," which is applied not to wicked demons, or to statues, or to animals, but (by those who know divine things) to what is truly divine and blessed; whereas the term "demons" is always applied to those wicked powers, freed from the encumbrance of a grosser body, who lead men astray, and fill them with distractions, and drag them down from God and supercelestial thoughts to things here below.

Chapter VI

He next proceeds to make the following statement about the Jews:—
"The first point relating to the Jews which is fitted to excite wonder, is that they should worship the heaven and the angels who dwell therein, and yet pass by and neglect its most venerable and powerful parts, as the sun, and moon, and the other heavenly bodies, both fixed stars and planets, as if it were possible that 'the whole' could be God, and yet its parts not divine; or [as if it were reasonable] to treat with the greatest respect those who are said to appear to such as are in darkness somewhere, blinded by some crooked sorcery, or dreaming dreams through the influence of shadowy spectres, [853] while those who prophesy so clearly and strikingly to all men, by means of whom rain, and heat, and clouds, and thunder (to which they offer worship), and lightnings, and fruits, and all kinds of productiveness, are brought about,—by means of whom God is revealed to them,—the most prominent heralds among those beings that are above,—those that are truly heavenly angels,—are to be regarded as of no account!" In making these statements, Celsus appears to have fallen into confusion, and to have penned them from false ideas of things which he did not understand; for it is patent to all who investigate the practices of the Jews, and compare them with those of the Christians, that the Jews who follow the law, which, speaking in the person of God, says, "Thou shalt have no other gods before me: thou shalt not make unto thee an image, nor a likeness of anything that is in heaven above, or that is in the earth beneath, or that is in the waters under the earth; thou shalt not bow down to them, nor serve them," [854] worship nothing else than the Supreme God, who made the heavens, and all things besides. Now it is evident that those who live according to the law, and worship the *Maker* of heaven, will not worship the heaven at the same time with God. Moreover, no one who obeys the law of Moses will bow down to the angels who are in heaven; and, in like manner, as they do not bow down to sun, moon, and stars, the host of heaven, they refrain also from doing obeisance to heaven and its angels, obeying the law which declares: "Lest thou lift up thine eyes to heaven, and when thou seest the sun, and the moon, and the stars, even all the host of heaven, shouldst be driven to worship them, and serve them, which the Lord thy God hath divided unto all nations." [855]

Chapter VII

Having, moreover, assumed that the Jews consider the heaven to be God, he adds that this is absurd; finding fault with those who bow down to the heaven, but not also to the sun, and moon, and stars, saying that the Jews do this, as if it were possible that "the whole" should be God, and its several parts not divine. And he seems to call the heaven "a whole," and sun, moon, and stars its several parts. Now, certainly neither Jews nor Christians call the "heaven" God. Let it be granted, however, that, as he alleges, the heaven *is* called God by the Jews, and suppose that sun, moon, and stars *are* parts of "heaven,"—which is by no means true, for neither are the animals and plants upon the earth any portion of it,—how is it true, even according to the opinions of the Greeks, that if God be a whole, His parts also are divine? Certainly they say that the Cosmos taken as the whole [856] is God, the Stoics calling it the First God, the followers of Plato the Second, and some of them the Third. According to these philosophers, then, seeing the whole Cosmos is God, its parts also are divine; so that not only are human beings divine, but the whole of the irrational creation, as being *"portions"* of the Cosmos; and besides these, the plants also are divine. And if the rivers, and mountains, and seas are portions of the Cosmos, then, since the whole Cosmos is God, are the rivers and seas also gods? But this even the Greeks will not assert. Those, however, who preside over rivers and seas (either demons or gods, as they call them), they would term gods. Now from this it follows that the general statement of Celsus, even according to the Greeks, who hold the doctrine of Providence, is false, that if any "whole" be a god, its parts necessarily are divine. But it follows from the doctrine of Celsus, that if the Cosmos be God, all that is in it is divine, being parts of the Cosmos. Now, according to this view, animals, as flies, and gnats, and worms, and every species of serpent, as well as of birds and fishes, will be divine,—an assertion which would not be made even by those who maintain that the Cosmos is God. But the Jews, who live according to the law of Moses, although they may not know how to receive the secret meaning of the law, which is conveyed in obscure language, will not maintain that either the heaven or the angels are God.

Chapter VIII

As we allege, however, that he has fallen into confusion in consequence of false notions which he has imbibed, come and let us point them out to the best of our ability, and show that although Celsus considers it to be a Jewish custom to bow down to the heaven and the angels in it, such a practice is not at all Jewish, but is in violation of Judaism, as it also is to do obeisance to sun, moon, and stars, as well as images. You will find at least in the book of Jeremiah the words of God censuring by the mouth of the prophet the Jewish people for doing obeisance to such objects, and for sacrificing to the queen of heaven, and to all the host of heaven. [857] The writings of the Christians, moreover, show, in censuring the sins committed among the Jews, that when God abandoned that people on account of certain sins, these sins [of idol-worship] also were committed by them. For it is related in the Acts of the Apostles regarding the Jews, that "God turned, and gave them up to worship the host of heaven; as it is written in the book of the prophets, O ye house of Israel, have ye offered to me slain beasts and sacrifices by the space of forty years in the wilderness? Yea, ye took up the tabernacle of Moloch, and the star of your god Remphan, figures which you made to worship them." [858] And in the writings of Paul, who was carefully trained in Jewish customs, and converted afterwards to Christianity by a miraculous appearance of Jesus, the following words may be read in the Epistle to the Colossians: "Let no man beguile you of your reward in a voluntary humility and worshipping of angels, intruding into those things which he hath not seen, vainly puffed up by his fleshly mind; and not holding the head, from which all the body by joint and bands having nourishment ministered, and knit together, increaseth with the increase of God." [859] But Celsus, having neither read these verses, nor having learned their contents from any other source, has represented, I know not how, the Jews as not transgressing their law in bowing down to the heavens, and to the angels therein.

Chapter IX

And still continuing a little confused, and not taking care to see what was relevant to the matter, he expressed his opinion that the Jews were induced by the incantations employed in jugglery and sorcery (in consequence of which certain phantoms appear, in obedience to the spells employed by the magicians) to bow down to the angels in heaven, not observing that this was contrary to their law, which said to them who practised such observances: "Regard not them which have familiar spirits, [860] neither seek after wizards, [861] to be defiled by them: I am the Lord your God." [862] He ought, therefore, either not to have at all attributed this practice to the Jews, seeing he has observed that they keep their law, and has called them "those who live according to their law;" or if he did attribute it, he ought to have shown that the Jews did this in violation of their code. But again, as they transgress their law who offer worship to those who are said to appear to them who are involved in darkness and blinded by sorcery, and who dream dreams, owing to obscure phantoms presenting themselves; so also do they transgress the law who offer sacrifice to sun, moon, and stars. [863] And there is thus great inconsistency in the same individual saying that the Jews are careful to keep their law by not bowing down to sun, and moon, and stars, while they are not so careful to keep it in the matter of heaven and the angels.

Chapter X

And if it be necessary for us to offer a defence of our refusal to recognise as gods, equally with angels, and sun, and moon, and stars, those who are called by the Greeks "manifest and visible" divinities, we shall answer that the law of Moses knows that these latter have been apportioned by God among all the nations under the heaven, but not amongst those who were selected by God as His chosen people above all the nations of the earth. For it is written in the book of Deuteronomy: "And lest thou lift up thine eyes unto heaven, and when thou seest the sun, and the moon, and the stars, even all the host of heaven, shouldst be driven to worship them, and serve them, which the Lord thy God hath divided unto all nations under the whole heaven. But the Lord hath taken us, and brought us forth out of the iron furnace, even out of Egypt, to be unto Him a people of inheritance, as ye are this day." [864] The Hebrew people, then, being called by God a "chosen generation, and a royal priesthood, and a holy nation, and a purchased people," [865] regarding whom it was foretold to Abraham by the voice of the Lord addressed to him, "Look now towards heaven, and tell the stars, if thou be able to number them: and He said unto him, So shall thy seed be;" [866] and having thus a hope that they would become as the stars of heaven, were not likely to bow down to those objects which they were to resemble as a result of their understanding and observing the law of God. For it was said to them: "The Lord our God hath multiplied us; and, behold, ye are this day as the stars of heaven for multitude." [867] In the book of Daniel, also, the following prophecies are found relating to those who are to share in the resurrection: "And at that time thy people shall be delivered, every one that has been written in the book. And many of them that sleep in the dust [868] of the earth shall awake; some to everlasting life, and some to shame and everlasting contempt. And they that be wise shall shine as the brightness of the firmament, and [those] of the many righteous [869] as the stars for ever and ever," [870] etc. And hence Paul, too, when speaking of the resurrection, says: "And there are also celestial bodies, and bodies terrestrial: but the glory of the celestial is one, and the glory of the terrestrial is another. There is one glory of the sun, and another glory of the moon, and another glory of the stars; for one star differeth from another star in glory. So also is the resurrection of the dead." [871] It was not therefore consonant to reason that those who had been taught sublimely [872] to ascend above all created things, and to hope for the enjoyment of the most glorious rewards with God on account of their virtuous lives, and who had heard the words, "Ye are the light of the world," [873] and, "Let your light so shine before men, that they, seeing your good works, may glorify your Father who is in heaven," [874] and who possessed through practice this brilliant and unfading wisdom, or who had secured even the "very reflection of everlasting light," [875] should be so impressed with the [mere] *visible* light of sun, and moon, and stars, that, on account of that sensible light of theirs, they should deem themselves (although possessed of so great a rational light of knowledge, and of the true light, and the light of the world, and the light of men) to be somehow inferior to them, and to bow down to them; seeing they ought to be worshipped, if they are to receive worship at all, not for the sake of the sensible light which is admired by the multitude, but because of the rational and true light, if indeed the stars in heaven are rational and virtuous beings, and have been illuminated with the light of knowledge by that wisdom which is the "reflection of everlasting light." For that sensible light of theirs is the work of the Creator of all things, while that rational light is derived perhaps from the principle of free-will within them. [876]

Chapter XI

But even this rational light itself ought not to be worshipped by him who beholds and understands the true light, by sharing in which these also are enlightened; nor by him who beholds God, the Father of the true light, — of whom it has been said, "God is light, and in Him there is no darkness at all." [877] Those, indeed, who worship sun, moon, and stars because their light is visible and celestial, would not bow down to a spark of fire or a lamp upon earth, because they see the incomparable superiority of those objects which are deemed worthy of homage to the light of sparks and lamps. So those who understand that God is light, and who have apprehended that the Son of God is "the true light which lighteth every man that cometh into the world," and who comprehend also how He says, "I am the light of the world," would not rationally offer worship to that which is, as it were, a spark in sun, moon, and stars, in comparison with God, who is light of the true light. Nor is it with a view to depreciate these great works of God's creative power, or to call them, after the fashion of Anaxagoras, "fiery masses," [878] that we thus speak of sun, and moon, and stars; but because we perceive the inexpressible superiority of the divinity of God, and that of His only-begotten Son, which surpasses all other things. And being persuaded that the sun himself, and moon, and stars pray to the Supreme God through His only-begotten Son, we judge it improper to pray to those beings who themselves offer up prayers [to God], seeing even they themselves would prefer that we should send up our requests to the God to whom they pray, rather than send them downwards to themselves, or apportion our power of prayer [879] between God and them. And here I may employ this illustration, as bearing upon this point: Our Lord and Saviour, hearing Himself on one occasion addressed as "Good Master," [880] referring him who used it to His own Father, said, "Why callest thou me good? There is none good but one, that is, God the Father." [881] And since it was in accordance with sound reason that this should be said by the Son of His Father's love, as being the image of the goodness of God, why should not the sun say with greater reason to those that bow down to him, Why do you worship me? "for thou wilt worship the Lord thy God, and Him only shalt thou serve;" [882] for it is He whom I and all who are with me serve and worship. And although one may not be so exalted [as the sun], nevertheless let such an one pray to the Word of God (who is able to heal him), and still more to His Father, who also to the righteous of former times "sent His word, and healed them, and delivered them from their destructions." [883]

Chapter XII

God accordingly, in His kindness, condescends to mankind, not in any local sense, but through His providence; [884] while the Son of God, not only [when on earth], but at *all* times, is with His own disciples, fulfilling the promise, "Lo, I am with you always, even to the end of the world." [885] And if a branch cannot bear fruit except it abide in the vine, it is evident that the disciples also of the Word, who are the rational branches of the Word's true vine, cannot produce the fruits of virtue unless they abide in the true vine, the Christ of God, who is with us locally here below upon the earth, and who is with those who cleave to Him in all parts of the world, and is also in all places with those who do not know Him. Another is made manifest by that John who wrote the Gospel, when, speaking in the person of John the Baptist, he said, "There standeth one among you whom ye know not; He it is who cometh after me." [886] And it is absurd, when He who fills heaven and earth, and who said, "Do I not fill heaven and earth? saith the Lord," [887] is with us, and near us (for I believe Him when He says, "I am a God nigh at hand, and not afar off, saith the Lord" [888]), to seek to pray to sun or moon, or one of the stars, whose influence does not reach the whole of the world. [889] But, to use the very words of Celsus, let it be granted that "the sun, moon, and stars *do* foretell rain, and heat, and clouds, and thunders," why, then, if they really do foretell such great things, ought we not rather to do homage to God, whose servant they are in uttering these predictions, and show reverence to *Him* rather than His *prophets*? Let them predict, then, the approach of lightnings, and fruits, and all manner of productions, and let all such things be under their administration; yet we shall not on that account worship those who themselves offer worship, as we do not worship even Moses, and those prophets who came from God after him, and who predicted better things than rain, and heat, and clouds, and thunders, and lightnings, and fruits, and all sorts of productions visible to the senses. Nay, even if sun, and moon, and stars were able to prophesy better things than rain, not even then shall we worship *them*, but the *Father* of the prophecies which are in them, and the *Word* of God, their minister. But grant that they are His heralds, and truly messengers of heaven, why, even then ought we not to worship the *God* whom they only proclaim and announce, rather than those who are the *heralds* and *messengers*?

Chapter XIII

Celsus, moreover, assumes that sun, and moon, and stars are regarded by us as of no account. Now, with regard to these, we acknowledge that they too are "waiting for the manifestation of the sons of God," being for the present subjected to the "vanity" of their material bodies, "by reason of Him who has subjected the same in hope." [890] But if Celsus had read the innumerable other passages where we speak of sun, moon, and stars, and especially these, — "Praise Him, all ye stars, and thou, O light," [891] and, "Praise Him, ye heaven of heavens," — he would not have said of us that we regard such mighty beings, which "greatly praise" the Lord God, as of no account. Nor did Celsus know the passage: "For the earnest expectation of the creature waiteth for the manifestation of the sons of God. For the creature was made subject to vanity, not willingly, but by reason of Him who hath subjected the same in hope; because the creature itself also shall be delivered from the bondage of corruption into the glorious liberty of the children of God." [892] And with these words let us terminate our defence against the charge of not worshipping sun, moon, and stars. And let us now bring forward those statements of his which follow, that we may, God willing, address to him in reply such arguments as shall be suggested by the light of truth.

Chapter XIV

The following, then, are his words: "It is folly on their part to suppose that when God, as if He were a cook, [893] introduces the fire [which is to consume the world], all the rest of the human race will be burnt up, while they alone will remain, not only such of them as are then alive, but also those who are long since dead, which latter will arise from the earth clothed with the self-same flesh [as during life]; for such a hope is simply one which might be cherished by worms. For what sort of human soul is that which would still long for a body that had been subject to corruption? Whence, also, this opinion of yours is not shared by some of the Christians, and they pronounce it to be exceedingly vile, and loathsome, and impossible; for what kind of body is that which, after being completely corrupted, can return to its original nature, and to that self-same first condition out of which it fell into dissolution? Being unable to return any answer, they betake themselves to a most absurd refuge, viz. that all things are possible to God. And yet God *cannot* do things that are disgraceful, nor does He wish to do things that are contrary to His nature; nor, if (in accordance with the wickedness of your own heart) you desired anything that was evil, would God accomplish it; nor must you believe at once that it will be done. For God does not rule the world in order to satisfy inordinate desires, or to allow disorder and confusion, but to govern a nature that is upright and just. [894] For the *soul*, indeed, He might be able to provide an everlasting life; while dead *bodies*, on the contrary, are, as Heraclitus observes, more worthless than dung. God, however, neither can nor will declare, contrary to all reason, that the flesh, which is full of those things which it is not even honourable to mention, is to exist for ever. For He is the reason of all things that exist, and therefore can do nothing either contrary to reason or contrary to Himself."

Chapter XV

Observe, now, here at the very beginning, how, in ridiculing the doctrine of a conflagration of the world, held by certain of the Greeks who have treated the subject in a philosophic spirit not to be depreciated, he would make us, "representing God, as it were, as a cook, hold the belief in a general conflagration;" not perceiving that, as certain Greeks were of opinion (perhaps having received their information from the ancient nation of the Hebrews), it is a purificatory fire which is brought upon the world, and probably also on each one of those who stand in need of chastisement by the fire and healing at the same time, seeing it *burns* indeed, but does not *consume*, those who are without a material body, [895] which needs to be consumed by that fire, and which burns and consumes those who by their actions, words, and thoughts have built up wood, or hay, or stubble, in that which is figuratively termed a "building." [896] And the Holy Scriptures say that the Lord will, like a refiner's fire and fuller's soap, [897] visit each one of those who require purification, because of the intermingling in them of a flood of wicked matter proceeding from their evil nature; who need fire, I mean, to refine, as it were, [the dross of] those who are intermingled with copper, and tin, and lead. And he who likes may learn this from the prophet Ezekiel. [898] But that we say that God brings fire upon the world, not like a cook, but like a God, who is the benefactor of them who stand in need of the discipline of fire, [899] will be testified by the prophet Isaiah, in whose writings it is related that a sinful nation was thus addressed: "Because thou hast coals of fire, sit upon them: they shall be to thee a help." [900] Now the Scripture is appropriately adapted to the multitudes of those who are to peruse it, because it speaks obscurely of things that are sad and gloomy, [901] in order to terrify those who cannot by any other means be saved from the flood of their sins, although even then the attentive reader will clearly discover the end that is to be accomplished by these sad and painful punishments upon those who endure them. It is sufficient, however, for the present to quote the words of Isaiah: "For my name's sake will I show mine anger, and my glory I will bring upon thee, that I may not destroy thee." [902] We have thus been under the necessity of referring in obscure terms to questions not fitted to the capacity of simple believers, who require a simpler instruction in words, that we might not appear to leave unrefuted the accusation of Celsus, that "God introduces the fire, [which is to destroy the world], as if He were a cook."

Chapter XVI

From what has been said, it will be manifest to intelligent hearers how we have to answer the following: "All the rest of the race will be completely burnt up, and they alone will remain." It is not to be wondered at, indeed, if such thoughts have been entertained by those amongst us who are called in Scripture the "foolish things" of the world, and "base things," and "things which are despised," and "things which are not," because "by the foolishness of preaching it pleased God to save them that believe on Him, after that, in the wisdom of God, the world by wisdom knew not God," [903] —because such individuals are unable to see distinctly the sense of each particular passage, [904] or unwilling to devote the necessary leisure to the investigation of Scripture, notwithstanding the injunction of Jesus, "Search the Scriptures." [905] The following, moreover, are his ideas regarding the fire which is to be brought upon the world by God, and the punishments which are to befall sinners. And perhaps, as it is appropriate to children that some things should be addressed to them in a manner befitting their infantile condition, to convert them, as being of very tender age, to a better course of life; so, to those whom the word terms "the foolish things of the world," and "the base," and "the despised," the just and obvious meaning of the passages relating to punishments is suitable, inasmuch as they cannot receive any other mode of conversion than that which is by fear and the presentation of punishment, and thus be saved from the many evils [which would befall them]. [906] The Scripture accordingly declares that only those who are unscathed by the fire and the punishments are to remain,— those, viz., whose opinions, and morals, and mind have been purified to the highest degree; while, on the other hand, those of a different nature— those, viz., who, according to their deserts, require the administration of punishment by fire—will be involved in these sufferings with a view to an end which it is suitable for God to bring upon those who have been created in His image, but who have lived in opposition to the will of that nature which is according to His image. And this is our answer to the statement, "All the rest of the race will be completely burnt up, but they alone are to remain."

Chapter XVII

Then, in the next place, having either himself misunderstood the sacred Scriptures, or those [interpreters] by whom they were not understood, he proceeds to assert that "it is said by us that there will remain at the time of the visitation which is to come upon the world by the fire of purification, not only those who are then alive, but also those who are long ago dead;" not observing that it is with a secret kind of wisdom that it was said by the apostle of Jesus: "We shall not all sleep, but we shall all be changed, in a moment, in the twinkling of an eye, at the last trump; for the trumpet shall sound, and the dead shall be raised incorruptible, and we shall be changed." [907] Now he ought to have noticed what was the meaning of him who uttered these words, as being one who was by no means dead, who made a distinction between himself and those like him and the dead, and who said afterwards, "The dead shall be raised incorruptible," and "we shall be changed." And as a proof that such was the apostle's meaning in writing those words which I have quoted from the First Epistle to the Corinthians, I will quote also from the First to the Thessalonians, in which Paul, as one who is alive and awake, and different from those who are asleep, speaks as follows: "For this we say unto you by the word of the Lord, that we who are alive and remain unto the coming of the Lord, shall not prevent them who are asleep; for the Lord Himself shall descend from heaven with a shout, with the voice of the archangel, and with the trump of God." [908] Then, again, after this, knowing that there were others dead in Christ besides himself and such as he, he subjoins the words, "The dead in Christ shall rise first; then we who are alive and remain shall be caught up together with them in the clouds, to meet the Lord in the air." [909]

Chapter XVIII

But since he has ridiculed at great length the doctrine of the resurrection of the flesh, which has been preached in the churches, and which is more clearly understood by the more intelligent believer; and as it is unnecessary again to quote his words, which have been already adduced, let us, with regard to the problem [910] (as in an apologetic work directed against an alien from the faith, and for the sake of those who are still "children, tossed to and fro, and carried about with every wind of doctrine, by the sleight of men, and cunning craftiness, whereby they lie in wait to deceive" [911]), state and establish to the best of our ability a few points expressly intended for our readers. Neither we, then, nor the Holy Scriptures, assert that with the same bodies, without a change to a higher condition, "shall those who were long dead arise from the earth and live again;" for in so speaking, Celsus makes a false charge against us. For we may listen to many passages of Scripture treating of the resurrection in a manner worthy of God, although it may suffice for the present to quote the language of Paul from the First Epistle to the Corinthians, where he says: "But some man will say, How are the dead raised up? and with what body do they come? Thou fool, that which thou sowest is not quickened, except it die. And that which thou sowest, thou sowest not that body that shall be, but bare grain, it may chance of wheat, or of some other grain; but God giveth it a body as it hath pleased Him, and to every seed his own body." [912] Now, observe how in these words he says that there is sown, "not that body that shall be;" but that of the body which is sown and cast naked into the earth (God giving to each seed its own body), there takes place as it were a resurrection: from the seed that was cast into the ground there arising a stalk, *e.g.* among such plants as the following, viz. the mustard plant, or of a larger tree, as in the olive, [913] or one of the fruit-trees.

Chapter XIX

God, then, gives to each thing its own body as He pleases: as in the case of plants that are sown, so also in the case of those beings who are, as it were, sown in dying, and who in due time receive, out of what has been "sown," the body assigned by God to each one according to his deserts. And we may hear, moreover, the Scripture teaching us at great length the difference between that which is, as it were, "sown," and that which is, as it were, "raised" from it, in these words: "It is sown in corruption, it is raised in incorruption; it is sown in dishonour, it is raised in glory; it is sown in weakness, it is raised in power; it is sown a natural body, it is raised a spiritual body." [914] And let him who has the capacity understand the meaning of the words: "As is the earthy, such are they also that are earthy; and as is the heavenly, such are they also that are heavenly. And as we have borne the image of the earthy, we shall also bear the image of the heavenly." [915] And although the apostle wished to conceal the secret meaning of the passage, which was not adapted to the simpler class of believers, and to the understanding of the common people, who are led by their faith to enter on a better course of life, he was nevertheless obliged afterwards to say (in order that we might not misapprehend his meaning), after "Let us bear the image of the heavenly," these words also: "Now this I say, brethren, that flesh and blood cannot inherit the kingdom of God; neither doth corruption inherit incorruption." [916] Then, knowing that there was a secret and mystical meaning in the passage, as was becoming in one who was leaving, in his epistles, to those who were to come after him words full of significance, he subjoins the following, "Behold, I show you a mystery;" [917] which is his usual style in introducing matters of a profounder and more mystical nature, and such as are fittingly concealed from the multitude, as is written in the book of Tobit: "It is good to keep close the secret of a king, but honourable to reveal the works of God," [918] —in a way consistent with truth and God's glory, and so as to be to the advantage of the multitude. Our hope, then, is *not* "the hope of worms, nor does our soul long for a body that has seen corruption;" for although it may require a body, for the sake of moving from place to place, [919] yet it understands (as having meditated on the wisdom [that is from above], agreeably to the declaration, "The mouth of the righteous will speak wisdom" [920]) the difference between the "earthly house," in which is the tabernacle of the building that is to be dissolved, and that in which the righteous do groan, being burdened,— not wishing to "put off" the tabernacle, but to be "clothed therewith," that by being clothed upon, mortality might be swallowed up of life. For, in virtue of the whole nature of the body being corruptible, the corruptible tabernacle must put on incorruption; and its other part, being mortal, and becoming liable to the death which follows sin, must put on immortality, in order that, when the corruptible shall have put on incorruption, and the mortal immortality, then shall come to pass what was predicted of old by the prophets,—the annihilation of the "victory" of death (because it had conquered and subjected us to his sway), and of its "sting," with which it stings the imperfectly defended soul, and inflicts upon it the wounds which result from sin.

Chapter XX

But since our views regarding the resurrection have, as far as time would permit, been stated in part on the present occasion (for we have systematically examined the subject in greater detail in other parts of our writings); and as now we must by means of sound reasoning refute the fallacies of Celsus, who neither understands the meaning of our Scripture, nor has the capacity of judging that the meaning of our wise men is not to be determined by those individuals who make no profession of anything more than of a [simple] faith in the Christian system, let us show that men, not to be lightly esteemed on account of their reasoning powers and dialectic subtleties, have given expression to very absurd [921] opinions. And if we must sneer [922] at them as contemptible old wives' fables, it is at them rather than at our narrative that we must sneer. The disciples of the Porch assert, that after a period of years there will be a conflagration of the world, and after that an arrangement of things in which everything will be unchanged, as compared with the former arrangement of the world. Those of them, however, who evinced their respect for this doctrine have said that there will be a change, although exceedingly slight, at the end of the cycle, from what prevailed during the preceding. And these men maintain, that in the succeeding cycle the same things will occur, and Socrates will be again the son of Sophroniscus, and a native of Athens; and Phænarete, being married to Sophroniscus, will again become his mother. And although they do not mention the word "resurrection," they show in reality that Socrates, who derived his origin from seed, will spring from that of Sophroniscus, and will be fashioned in the womb of Phænarete; and being brought up at Athens, will practise the study of philosophy, as if his former philosophy had arisen again, and were to be in no respect different from what it was before. Anytus and Melitus, too, will arise again as accusers of Socrates, and the Council of Areopagus will condemn him to death! But what is more ridiculous still, is that Socrates will clothe himself with garments not at all different from those which he wore during the former cycle, and will live in the same unchanged state of poverty, and in the same unchanged city of Athens! And Phalaris will again play the tyrant, and his brazen bull will pour forth its bellowings from the voices of victims within, unchanged from those who were condemned in the former cycle! And Alexander of Pheræ, too, will again act the tyrant with a cruelty unaltered from the former time, and will condemn to death the same "unchanged" individuals as before. But what need is there to go into detail upon the doctrine held by the Stoic philosophers on such things, and which escapes the ridicule of Celsus, and is perhaps even venerated by him, since he regards Zeno as a wiser man than Jesus?

Chapter XXI

The disciples of Pythagoras, too, and of Plato, although they appear to hold the incorruptibility of the world, yet fall into similar errors. For as the planets, after certain definite cycles, assume the same positions, and hold the same relations to one another, all things on earth will, they assert, be like what they were at the time when the same state of planetary relations existed in the world. From this view it necessarily follows, that when, after the lapse of a lengthened cycle, the planets come to occupy towards each other the same relations which they occupied in the time of Socrates, Socrates will again be born of the same parents, and suffer the same treatment, being accused by Anytus and Melitus, and condemned by the Council of Areopagus! The learned among the Egyptians, moreover, hold similar views, and yet they are treated with respect, and do not incur the ridicule of Celsus and such as he; while we, who maintain that all things are administered by God in proportion to the relation of the free-will of each individual, and are ever being brought into a better condition, so far as they admit of being so, [923] and who know that the nature of our free-will admits of the occurrence of contingent events [924] (for it is incapable of receiving the wholly unchangeable character of God), yet do not appear to say anything worthy of a testing examination.

Chapter XXII

Let no one, however, suspect that, in speaking as we do, we belong to those who are indeed called Christians, but who set aside the doctrine of the resurrection as it is taught in Scripture. For these persons cannot, so far as their principles apply, at all establish that the stalk or tree which springs up comes from the grain of wheat, or anything else [which was cast into the ground]; whereas we, who believe that that which is "sown" is not "quickened" unless it die, and that there is sown not that body that shall be (for God gives it a body as it pleases Him, raising it in incorruption after it is sown in corruption; and after it is sown in dishonour, raising it in glory; and after it is sown in weakness, raising it in power; and after it is sown a natural body, raising it a spiritual),—we preserve both the doctrine [925] of the church of Christ and the grandeur of the divine promise, proving also the possibility of its accomplishment not by mere assertion, but by arguments; knowing that although heaven and earth, and the things that are in them, may pass away, yet His words regarding each individual thing, being, as parts of a whole, or species of a genus, the utterances of Him who was God the Word, who was in the beginning with God, shall by no means pass away. For we desire to listen to Him who said: "Heaven and earth shall pass away, but my words shall not pass away." [926]

Chapter XXIII

We, therefore, do not maintain that the body which has undergone corruption resumes its original nature, any more than the grain of wheat which has decayed returns to its former condition. But we do maintain, that as above the grain of wheat there arises a stalk, so a certain power [927] is implanted in the body, which is not destroyed, and from which the body is raised up in incorruption. The philosophers of the Porch, however, in consequence of the opinions which they hold regarding the unchangeableness of things after a certain cycle, assert that the body, after undergoing complete corruption, will return to its original condition, and will again assume that first nature from which it passed into a state of dissolution, establishing these points, as they think, by irresistible arguments. [928] We, however, do not betake ourselves to a most absurd refuge, saying that with God *all* things are possible; for we know how to understand this word "all" as not referring either to things that are "non-existent" or that are inconceivable. But we maintain, at the same time, that God cannot do what is disgraceful, since then He would be capable of ceasing to be God; for if He do anything that is disgraceful, He is not God. Since, however, he lays it down as a principle, that "God does not desire what is contrary to nature," we have to make a distinction, and say that if any one asserts that wickedness is contrary to nature, while we maintain that "God does not desire what is contrary to nature,"—either what springs from wickedness or from an irrational principle,—yet, if such things happen according to the word and will of God, we must at once necessarily hold that they are not contrary to nature. Therefore things which are done by God, although they may be, or may *appear* to some to be incredible, are not contrary to nature. And if we must press the force of words, [929] we would say that, in comparison with what is generally understood as "nature," there *are* certain things which are *beyond* its power, which God could at any time do; as, *e.g.,* in raising man above the level of human nature, and causing him to pass into a better and more divine condition, and preserving him in the same, so long as he who is the object of His care shows by his actions that he desires [the continuance of His help].

Chapter XXIV

Moreover, as we have already said that for God to desire anything unbecoming Himself would be destructive of His existence as Deity, we will add that if man, agreeably to the wickedness of his nature, should desire anything that is abominable, [930] God cannot grant it. And now it is from no spirit of contention that we answer the assertions of Celsus; but it is in the spirit of truth that we investigate them, as assenting to his view that "He is the God, not of inordinate desires, nor of error and disorder, but of a nature just and upright," because He is the source of all that is good. And that He is able to provide an eternal life for the soul we acknowledge; and that He possesses not only the "power," but the "will." In view, therefore, of these considerations, we are not at all distressed by the assertion of Heraclitus, adopted by Celsus, that "dead bodies are to be cast out as more worthless than dung;" and yet, with reference even to this, one might say that dung, indeed, ought to be cast out, while the dead bodies of men, on account of the soul by which they were inhabited, especially if it had been virtuous, ought not to be cast out. For, in harmony with those laws which are based upon the principles of equity, bodies are deemed worthy of sepulture, with the honours accorded on such occasions, that no insult, so far as can be helped, may be offered to the soul which dwelt within, by casting forth the body (after the soul has departed) like that of the animals. Let it not then be held, contrary to reason, that it is the will of God to declare that the grain of wheat is not immortal, but the stalk which springs from it, while the body which is sown in corruption is not, but that which is raised by Him in incorruption. But according to Celsus, God Himself is the reason of all things, while according to our view it is His Son, of whom we say in philosophic language, "In the beginning was the Word, and the Word was with God, and the Word was God;" [931] while in our judgment also, God cannot do anything which is contrary to reason, or contrary to Himself.

Chapter XXV

Let us next notice the statements of Celsus, which follow the preceding, and which are as follow: "As the Jews, then, became a peculiar people, and enacted laws in keeping with the customs of their country, [932] and maintain them up to the present time, and observe a mode of worship which, whatever be its nature, is yet derived from their fathers, they act in these respects like other men, because each nation retains its ancestral customs, whatever they are, if they happen to be established among them. And such an arrangement appears to be advantageous, not only because it has occurred to the mind of other nations to decide some things differently, but also because it is a duty to protect what has been established for the public advantage; and also because, in all probability, the various quarters of the earth were from the beginning allotted to different superintending spirits, [933] and were thus distributed among certain governing powers, [934] and in this manner the administration of the world is carried on. And whatever is done among each nation in this way would be rightly done, wherever it was agreeable to the wishes [of the superintending powers], while it would be an act of impiety to get rid of [935] the institutions established from the beginning in the various places." By these words Celsus shows that the Jews, who were formerly Egyptians, subsequently became a "peculiar people," and enacted laws which they carefully preserve. And not to repeat his statements, which have been already before us, he says that it is advantageous to the Jews to observe their ancestral worship, as other nations carefully attend to theirs. And he further states a deeper reason why it is of advantage to the Jews to cultivate their ancestral customs, in hinting dimly that those to whom was allotted the office of superintending the country which was being legislated for, enacted the laws of each land in co-operation with its legislators. He appears, then, to indicate that both the country of the Jews, and the nation which inhabits it, are superintended by one or more beings, who, whether they were one or more, co-operated with Moses, and enacted the laws of the Jews.

Chapter XXVI

"We must," he says, "observe the laws, not only because it has occurred to the mind of others to decide some things differently, but because it is a duty to protect what has been enacted for the public advantage, and also because, in all probability, the various quarters of the earth were from the beginning allotted to different superintending spirits, and were distributed among certain governing powers, and in this manner the administration of the world is carried on." Thus Celsus, as if he had forgotten what he had said against the Jews, now includes them in the general eulogy which he passes upon all who observe their ancestral customs, remarking: "And whatever is done among each nation in this way, would be rightly done whenever agreeable to the wishes [of the superintendents]." And observe here, whether he does not openly, so far as he can, express a wish that the Jew should live in the observance of his own laws, and not depart from them, because he would commit an act of impiety if he apostatized; for his words are: "It would be an act of impiety to get rid of the institutions established from the beginning in the various places." Now I should like to ask him, and those who entertain his views, who it was that distributed the various quarters of the earth from the beginning among the different superintending spirits; and especially, who gave the country of the Jews, and the Jewish people themselves, to the one or more superintendents to whom it was allotted? Was it, as Celsus would say, Jupiter who assigned the Jewish people and their country to a certain spirit or spirits? And was it *his* wish, to whom they were thus assigned, to enact among them the laws which prevail, or was it *against* his will that it was done? You will observe that, whatever be his answer, he is in a strait. But if the various quarters of the earth were *not* allotted by some one being to the various superintending spirits, then each one at random, and without the superintendence of a higher power, divided the earth according to chance; and yet such a view is absurd, and destructive in no small degree of the providence of the God who presides over all things.

Chapter XXVII

Any one, indeed, who chooses, may relate how the various quarters of the earth, being distributed among certain governing powers, are administered by those who superintend them; but let him tell us also how what is done among each nation is done rightly when agreeable to the wishes of the superintendents. Let him, for example, tell us whether the laws of the Scythians, which permit the murder of parents, are right laws; or those of the Persians, which do not forbid the marriages of sons with their mothers, or of daughters with their own fathers. But what need is there for me to make selections from those who have been engaged in the business of enacting laws among the different nations, and to inquire how the laws are rightly enacted among each, according as they please the superintending powers? Let Celsus, however, tell us how it would be an act of impiety to get rid of those ancestral laws which permit the marriages of mothers and daughters; or which pronounce a man happy who puts an end to his life by hanging, or declare that they undergo entire purification who deliver themselves over to the fire, and who terminate their existence by fire; and how it is an act of impiety to do away with those laws which, for example, prevail in the Tauric Chersonese, regarding the offering up of strangers in sacrifice to Diana, or among certain of the Libyan tribes regarding the sacrifice of children to Saturn. Moreover, this inference follows from the dictum of Celsus, that it is an act of impiety on the part of the Jews to do away with those ancestral laws which forbid the worship of any other deity than the Creator of all things. And it will follow, according to his view, that piety is not divine by its own nature, but by a certain [external] arrangement and appointment. For it is an act of piety among certain tribes to worship a crocodile, and to eat what is an object of adoration among other tribes; while, again, with others it is a pious act to worship a calf, and among others, again, to regard the goat as a god. And, in this way, the same individual will be regarded as acting piously according to one set of laws, and impiously according to another; and this is the most absurd result that can be conceived!

Chapter XXVIII

It is probable, however, that to such remarks as the above, the answer returned would be, that he was pious who kept the laws of his *own* country, and not at all chargeable with impiety for the non-observance of those of *other* lands; and that, again, he who was deemed guilty of impiety among certain nations was not really so, when he worshipped his own gods, agreeably to his country's laws, although he made war against, and even feasted on, [936] those who were regarded as divinities among those nations which possessed laws of an opposite kind. Now, observe here whether these statements do not exhibit the greatest confusion of mind regarding the nature of what is just, and holy, and religious; since there is no accurate definition laid down of these things, nor are they described as having a peculiar character of their own, and stamping as religious those who act according to their injunctions. If, then, religion, and piety, and righteousness belong to those things which are so only by comparison, so that the same act may be both pious and impious, according to different relations and different laws, see whether it will not follow that temperance [937] also is a thing of comparison, and courage as well, and prudence, and the other virtues, than which nothing could be more absurd! What we have said, however, is sufficient for the more general and simple class of answers to the allegations of Celsus. But as we think it likely that some of those who are accustomed to deeper investigation will fall in with this treatise, let us venture to lay down some considerations of a profounder kind, conveying a mystical and secret view respecting the original distribution of the various quarters of the earth among different superintending spirits; and let us prove to the best of our ability, that our doctrine is free from the absurd consequences enumerated above.

Chapter XXIX

It appears to me, indeed, that Celsus has misunderstood some of the deeper reasons relating to the arrangement of terrestrial affairs, some of which are touched upon [938] even in Grecian history, when certain of those who are considered to be gods are introduced as having contended with each other about the possession of Attica; while in the writings of the Greek poets also, some who are called gods are represented as acknowledging that certain places here are preferred by them [939] before others. The history of barbarian nations, moreover, and especially that of Egypt, contains some such allusions to the division of the so-called Egyptian nomes, when it states that Athena, who obtained Saïs by lot, is the same who also has possession of Attica. And the learned among the Egyptians can enumerate innumerable instances of this kind, although I do not know whether they include the Jews and their country in this division. And now, so far as testimonies outside the word of God bearing on this point are concerned, enough have been adduced for the present. We say, moreover, that our prophet of God and His genuine servant Moses, in his song in the book of Deuteronomy, makes a statement regarding the portioning out of the earth in the following terms: "When the Most High divided the nations, when He dispersed the sons of Adam, He set the bounds of the people according to the number of the angels of God; and the Lord's portion was His people Jacob, and Israel the cord of His inheritance." [940] And regarding the distribution of the nations, the same Moses, in his work entitled Genesis, thus expresses himself in the style of a historical narrative: "And the whole earth was of one language and of one speech; and it came to pass, as they journeyed from the east, that they found a plain in the land of Shinar, and they dwelt there." [941] A little further on he continues: "And the Lord came down to see the city and the tower, which the children of men had built. And the Lord said, Behold, the people is one, and they have all one language; and this they have begun to do: and now nothing will be restrained from them which they have imagined to do. Go to, let us go down, and there confound their language, that they may not understand one another's speech. And the Lord scattered them abroad from thence upon the face of all the earth: and they left off to build the city and the tower. Therefore is the name of it called Confusion; [942] because the Lord did there confound the language of all the earth:

and from thence did the Lord scatter them abroad upon the face of all the earth." [943] In the treatise of Solomon, moreover, on "Wisdom," and on the events at the time of the confusion of languages, when the division of the earth took place, we find the following regarding Wisdom: "Moreover, the nations. in their wicked conspiracy being confounded, she found out the righteous, and preserved him blameless unto God, and kept him strong in his tender compassion towards his son." [944] But on these subjects much, and that of a mystical kind, might be said; in keeping with which is the following: "It is good to keep close the secret of a king," [945] —in order that the doctrine of the entrance of souls into bodies (not, however, that of the transmigration from one body into another) may not be thrown before the common understanding, nor what is holy given to the dogs, nor pearls be cast before swine. For such a procedure would be impious, being equivalent to a betrayal of the mysterious declarations of God's wisdom, of which it has been well said: "Into a malicious soul wisdom shall not enter, nor dwell in a body subject to sin." [946] It is sufficient, however, to represent in the style of a historic narrative what is intended to convey a secret meaning in the garb of history, that those who have the capacity may work out for themselves all that relates to the subject.

Chapter XXX

[The narrative, then, may be understood as follows.] All the people upon the earth are to be regarded as having used one divine language, and so long as they lived harmoniously together were preserved in the use of this divine language, and they remained without moving from the east so long as they were imbued with the sentiments of the "light," and of the "reflection" of the eternal light. [947] But when they departed from the east, and began to entertain sentiments alien to those of the east, [948] they found a place in the land of Shinar (which, when interpreted, means "gnashing of teeth," by way of indicating symbolically that they had lost the means of their support), and in it they took up their abode. Then, desiring to gather together material things, [949] and to join to heaven what had no natural affinity for it, that by means of material things they might conspire against such as were immaterial, they said, "Come, let us make bricks, and burn them with fire." Accordingly, when they had hardened and compacted these materials of clay and matter, and had shown their desire to make brick into stone, and clay into bitumen, and by these means to build a city and a tower, the head of which was, at least in their conception, to reach up to the heavens, after the manner of the "high things which exalt themselves against the knowledge of God," each one was handed over (in proportion to the greater or less departure from the east which had taken place among them, and in proportion to the extent in which bricks had been converted into stones, and clay into bitumen, and building carried on out of these materials) to angels of character more or less severe, and of a nature more or less stern, until they had paid the penalty of their daring deeds; and they were conducted by those angels, who imprinted on each his native language, to the different parts of the earth according to their deserts: some, for example, to a region of burning heat, others to a country which chastises its inhabitants by its cold; others, again, to a land exceedingly difficult of cultivation, others to one less so in degree; while a fifth were brought into a land filled with wild beasts, and a sixth to a country comparatively free of these.

Chapter XXXI

Now, in the next place, if any one has the capacity, let him understand that in what assumes the form of history, and which contains some things that are literally true, while yet it conveys a deeper meaning, those who preserved their original language continued, by reason of their not having migrated from the east, in possession of the east, and of their eastern language. And let him notice, that these alone became the portion of the Lord, and His people who were called Jacob, and Israel the cord of His inheritance; and these alone were governed by a ruler who did not receive those who were placed under him for the purpose of punishment, as was the case with the others. Let him also, who has the capacity to perceive as far as mortals may, observe that in the body politic [950] of those who were assigned to the Lord as His pre-eminent portion, sins were committed, first of all, such as might be forgiven, and of such a nature as not to make the sinner worthy of entire desertion, while subsequently they became more numerous, though still of a nature to be pardoned. And while remarking that this state of matters continued for a considerable time, and that a remedy was always applied, and that after certain intervals these persons returned to their duty, let him notice that they were given over, in proportion to their transgressions, to those to whom had been assigned the other quarters of the earth; and that, after being at first slightly punished, and having made atonement, [951] they returned, as if they had undergone discipline, [952] to their proper habitations. Let him notice also that afterwards they were delivered over to rulers of a severer character—to Assyrians and Babylonians, as the Scriptures would call them. In the next place, notwithstanding that means of healing were being applied, let him observe that they were still multiplying their transgressions, and that they were on that account dispersed into other regions by the rulers of the nations that oppressed them. And their own ruler intentionally overlooked their oppression at the hands of the rulers of the other nations, in order that he also with good reason, as avenging himself, having obtained power to tear away from the other nations as many as he can, may do so, and enact for them laws, and point out a manner of life agreeably to which they ought to live, that so he may conduct them to the end to which those of the former people were conducted who did not commit sin.

Chapter XXXII

And by this means let those who have the capacity of comprehending truths so profound, learn that he to whom were allotted those who had not formerly sinned is far more powerful than the others, since he has been able to make a selection of individuals from the portion of the whole, [953] and to separate them from those who received them for the purpose of punishment, and to bring them under the influence of laws, and of a mode of life which helps to produce an oblivion of their former transgressions. But, as we have previously observed, these remarks are to be understood as being made by us with a concealed meaning, by way of pointing out the mistakes of those who asserted that "the various quarters of the earth were from the beginning distributed among different superintending spirits, and being allotted among certain governing powers, were administered in this way;" from which statement Celsus took occasion to make the remarks referred to. But since those who wandered away from the east were delivered over, on account of their sins, to "a reprobate mind," and to "vile affections," and to "uncleanness through the lusts of their own hearts," [954] in order that, being sated with sin, they might hate it, we shall refuse our assent to the assertion of Celsus, that "because of the superintending spirits distributed among the different parts of the earth, what is done among each nation is rightly done;" for our desire is to do what is *not* agreeable to these spirits. [955] For we see that it is a religious act to do away with the customs originally established in the various places by means of laws of a better and more divine character, which were enacted by Jesus, as one possessed of the greatest power, who has rescued us "from the present evil world," and "from the princes of the world that come to nought;" and that it is a mark of irreligion not to throw ourselves at the feet of Him who has manifested Himself to be holier and more powerful than all other rulers, and to whom God said, as the prophets many generations before predicted: "Ask of me, and I shall give Thee the heathen for Thine inheritance, and the uttermost parts of the earth for Thy possession." [956] For He, too, has become the "expectation" of us who from among the heathen have believed upon Him, and upon His Father, who is God over all things.

Chapter XXXIII

The remarks which we have made not only answer the statements of Celsus regarding the superintending spirits, but anticipate in some measure what he afterwards brings forward, when he says: "Let the second party come forward; and I shall ask them whence they come, and whom they regard as the originator of their ancestral customs. They will reply, No one, because they spring from the same source as the Jews themselves, and derive their instruction and superintendence [957] from no other quarter, and notwithstanding they have revolted from the Jews." Each one of us, then, is come "in the last days," when one Jesus has visited us, to the "visible mountain of the Lord," the Word that is above every word, and to the "house of God," which is "the church of the living God, the pillar and ground of the truth." [958] And we notice how it is built upon "the tops of the mountains," *i.e.* the predictions of all the prophets, which are its foundations. And this house is exalted above the hills, *i.e.* those individuals among men who make a profession of superior attainments in wisdom and truth; and all the nations come to it, and the "many nations" go forth, and say to one another, turning to the religion which in the last days has shone forth through Jesus Christ: "Come ye, and let us go up to the mountain of the Lord, to the house of the God of Jacob; and He will teach us of His ways, and we will walk in them." [959] For the law came forth from the dwellers in Sion, and settled among us as a spiritual law. Moreover, the word of the Lord came forth from that very Jerusalem, that it might be disseminated through all places, and might judge in the midst of the heathen, selecting those whom it sees to be submissive, and rejecting [960] the disobedient, who are many in number. And to those who inquire of us whence we come, or who is our founder, [961] we reply that we are come, agreeably to the counsels of Jesus, to "cut down our hostile and insolent 'wordy' [962] swords into ploughshares, and to convert into pruning-hooks the spears formerly employed in war." [963] For we no longer take up "sword against nation," nor do we "learn war any more," having become children of peace, for the sake of Jesus, who is our leader, instead of those whom our fathers followed, among whom we were "strangers to the covenant," and having received a law, for which we give thanks to Him that rescued us from the error [of our ways], saying, "Our fathers honoured lying idols, and there is not among them one that causeth it to rain." [964] Our Superintendent, then, and Teacher, having come forth from the Jews, regulates the whole world by the word of His teaching. And having made these remarks by way of anticipation, we have refuted as well as we could the untrue statements of Celsus, by subjoining the appropriate answer.

Chapter XXXIV

But, that we may not pass without notice what Celsus has said between these and the preceding paragraphs, let us quote his words: "We might adduce Herodotus as a witness on this point, for he expresses himself as follows: 'For the people of the cities Marea and Apis, who inhabit those parts of Egypt that are adjacent to Libya, and who look upon themselves as Libyans, and not as Egyptians, finding their sacrificial worship oppressive, and wishing not to be excluded from the use of cows' flesh, sent to the oracle of Jupiter Ammon, saying that there was no relationship between them and the Egyptians, that they dwelt outside the Delta, that there was no community of sentiment between them and the Egyptians, and that they wished to be allowed to partake of all kinds of food. But the god would not allow them to do as they desired, saying that that country was a part of Egypt, which was watered by the inundation of the Nile, and that those were Egyptians who dwell to the south of the city of Elephantine, and drink of the river Nile.' [965] Such is the narrative of Herodotus. But," continues Celsus, "Ammon in divine things would not make a worse ambassador than the angels of the Jews, [966] so that there is nothing wrong in each nation observing its established method of worship. Of a truth, we shall find very great differences prevailing among the nations, and yet each seems to deem its own by far the best. Those inhabitants of Ethiopia who dwell in Meroe worship Jupiter and Bacchus alone; the Arabians, Urania and Bacchus only; all the Egyptians, Osiris and Isis; the Saïtes, Minerva; while the Naucratites have recently classed Serapis among their deities, and the rest according to their respective laws. And some abstain from the flesh of sheep, and others from that of crocodiles; others, again, from that of cows, while they regard swine's flesh with loathing. The Scythians, indeed, regard it as a noble act to banquet upon human beings. Among the Indians, too, there are some who deem themselves discharging a holy duty in eating their fathers, and this is mentioned in a certain passage by Herodotus. For the sake of credibility, I shall again quote his very words, for he writes as follows: 'For if any one were to make this proposal to all men, viz. to bid him select out of all existing laws the best, each would choose, after examination, those of his own country. Men each consider their own laws much the best, and therefore it is not likely that any other than a madman would make these things a subject of ridicule. But that such are the conclusions of all men regarding the laws, may be determined by many other evidences, and especially by the following illustration. Darius, during his reign, having summoned before him those Greeks who happened to be present at the time, inquired of them for how much they would be willing to eat their deceased fathers; their answer was, that for no consideration would they do such a thing. After this, Darius summoned those Indians who are called Callatians, who are in the habit of eating their parents, and asked of them in the presence of these Greeks, who learned what passed through an interpreter, for what amount of money they would undertake to burn their deceased fathers with fire; on which they raised a loud shout, and bade the king say no more.' [967] Such is the way, then, in which these matters are regarded. And Pindar appears to me to be right in saying that 'law' is the king of all things." [968]

Chapter XXXV

The argument of Celsus appears to point by these illustrations to this conclusion: that it is "an obligation incumbent on all men to live according to their country's customs, in which case they will escape censure; whereas the Christians, who have abandoned their native usages, and who are not one nation like the Jews, are to be blamed for giving their adherence to the teaching of Jesus." Let him then tell us whether it is a becoming thing for philosophers, and those who have been taught not to yield to superstition, to abandon their country's customs, so as to eat of those articles of food which are prohibited in their respective cities? or whether this proceeding of theirs is opposed to what is becoming? For if, on account of their philosophy, and the instructions which they have received against superstition, they should eat, in disregard of their native laws, what was interdicted by their fathers, why should the Christians (since the gospel requires *them* not to busy themselves about statues and images, or even about any of the created works of God, but to ascend on high, and present the soul to the Creator), when acting in a similar manner to the philosophers, be censured for so doing? But if, for the sake of defending the theses which he has proposed to himself, Celsus, or those who think with him, should say, that even one who had studied philosophy would keep his country's laws, then philosophers in Egypt, for example, would act most ridiculously in avoiding the eating of onions, in order to observe their country's laws, or certain parts of the body, as the head and shoulders, in order not to transgress the traditions of their fathers. And I do not speak of those Egyptians who shudder with fear at the discharge of wind from the body, because if any one of these were to become a philosopher, and still observe the laws of his country, he would be a ridiculous philosopher, acting very unphilosophically. [969] In the same way, then, he who has been led by the gospel to worship the God of all things, and, from regard to his country's laws, lingers here below among images and statues of men, and does not desire to ascend to the Creator, will resemble those who have indeed learned philosophy, but who are afraid of things which ought to inspire no terrors, and who regard it as an act of impiety to eat of those things which have been enumerated.

Chapter XXXVI

But what sort of being is this Ammon of Herodotus, whose words Celsus has quoted, as if by way of demonstrating how each one ought to keep his country's laws? For this Ammon would not allow the people of the cities of Marea and Apis, who inhabit the districts adjacent to Libya, to treat as a matter of indifference the use of cows' flesh, which is a thing not only indifferent in its own nature, but which does not prevent a man from being noble and virtuous. If Ammon, then, forbade the use of cows' flesh, because of the advantage which results from the use of the animal in the cultivation of the ground, and in addition to this, because it is by the female that the breed is increased, the account would possess more plausibility. But now he simply requires that those who drink of the Nile should observe the laws of the Egyptians regarding kine. And hereupon Celsus, taking occasion to pass a jest upon the employment of the angels among the Jews as the ambassadors of God, says that "Ammon did not make a worse ambassador of divine things than did the angels of the Jews," into the meaning of whose words and manifestations he instituted no investigation; otherwise he would have seen, that it is not for oxen that God is concerned, even where He may appear to legislate for them, or for irrational animals, but that what is written for the sake of men, under the appearance of relating to irrational animals, contains certain truths of nature. [970] Celsus, moreover, says that no wrong is committed by any one who wishes to observe the religious worship sanctioned by the laws of his country; and it follows, according to his view, that the Scythians commit no wrong, when, in conformity with their country's laws, they eat human beings. And those Indians who eat their own fathers are considered, according to Celsus, to do a religious, or at least not a wicked act. He adduces, indeed, a statement of Herodotus which favours the principle that each one ought, from a sense of what is becoming, to obey his country's laws; and he appears to approve of the custom of those Indians called Callatians, who in the time of Darius devoured their parents, since, on Darius inquiring for how great a sum of money they would be willing to lay aside this usage, they raised a loud shout, and bade the king say no more.

Chapter XXXVII

As there are, then, generally two laws presented to us, the one being the law of nature, of which God would be the legislator, and the other being the written law of cities, it is a proper thing, when the written law is not opposed to that of God, for the citizens not to abandon it under pretext of foreign customs; but when the law of nature, that is, the law of God, commands what is opposed to the written law, observe whether reason will not tell us to bid a long farewell to the written code, and to the desire of its legislators, and to give ourselves up to the legislator God, and to choose a life agreeable to His word, although in doing so it may be necessary to encounter dangers, and countless labours, and even death and dishonour. For when there are some laws in harmony with the will of God, which are opposed to others which are in force in cities, and when it is impracticable to please God (and those who administer laws of the kind referred to), it would be absurd to contemn those acts by means of which we may please the Creator of all things, and to select those by which we shall become displeasing to God, though we may satisfy unholy laws, and those who love them. But since it is reasonable in other matters to prefer the law of nature, which is the law of God, before the written law, which has been enacted by men in a spirit of opposition to the law of God, why should we not do this still more in the case of those laws which relate to God? Neither shall we, like the Ethiopians who inhabit the parts about Meroe, worship, as is their pleasure, Jupiter and Bacchus only; nor shall we at all reverence Ethiopian gods in the Ethiopian manner; nor, like the Arabians, shall we regard Urania and Bacchus alone as divinities; nor in any degree at all deities in which the difference of sex has been a ground of distinction (as among the Arabians, who worship Urania as a female, and Bacchus as a male deity); nor shall we, like all the Egyptians, regard Osiris and Isis as gods; nor shall we enumerate Athena among these, as the Saïtes are pleased to do. And if to the ancient inhabitants of Naucratis it seemed good to worship other divinities, while their modern descendants have begun quite recently to pay reverence to Serapis, who never was a god at all, we shall not on that account assert that a new being who was not formerly a god, nor at all known to men, is a deity. For the Son of God, "the First-born of all creation," although He seemed recently to have become incarnate, is not by any means on that account recent. For the Holy Scriptures know Him to be the most ancient of all the works of creation; [971] for it was to Him that God said regarding the creation of man, "Let us make man in our image, after our likeness." [972]

Chapter XXXVIII

I wish, however, to show how Celsus asserts without any good reason, that each one reveres his domestic and native institutions. For he declares that "those Ethiopians who inhabit Meroe know only of two gods, Jupiter and Bacchus, and worship these alone; and that the Arabians also know only of two, viz. Bacchus, who is also an Ethiopian deity, and Urania, whose worship is confined to them." According to his account, neither do the Ethiopians worship Urania, nor the Arabians Jupiter. If, then, an Ethiopian were from any accident to fall into the hands of the Arabians, and were to be judged guilty of impiety because he did not worship Urania, and for this reason should incur the danger of death, would it be proper for the Ethiopian to die, or to act contrary to his country's laws, and do obeisance to Urania? Now, if it would be proper for him to act contrary to the laws of his country, he will do what is not right, so far as the language of Celsus is any standard; while, if he should be led away to death, let him show the reasonableness of selecting such a fate. I know not whether, if the Ethiopian doctrine taught men to philosophize on the immortality of the soul, and the honour which is paid to religion, they would reverence those as deities who are deemed to be such by the laws of the country. [973] A similar illustration may be employed in the case of the Arabians, if from any accident they happened to visit the Ethiopians about Meroe. For, having been taught to worship Urania and Bacchus alone, they will not worship Jupiter along with the Ethiopians; and if, adjudged guilty of impiety, they should be led away to death, let Celsus tell us what it would be reasonable on their part to do. And with regard to the fables which relate to Osiris and Isis, it is superfluous and out of place at present to enumerate them. For although an allegorical meaning may be given to the fables, they will nevertheless teach us to offer divine worship to cold water, and to the earth, which is subject to men, and all the animal creation. For in this way, I presume, they refer Osiris to water, and Isis to earth; while with regard to Serapis the accounts are numerous and conflicting, to the effect that very recently he appeared in public, agreeably to certain juggling tricks performed at the desire of Ptolemy, who wished to show to the people of Alexandria as it were a visible god. And we have read in the writings of Numenius the Pythagorean regarding his formation, that he partakes of the essence of all the animals and plants that are under the control of nature, that he may appear to have been fashioned into a god, not by the makers of images alone, with the aid of profane mysteries, and juggling tricks employed to invoke demons, but also by magicians and sorcerers, and those demons who are bewitched by their incantations. [974]

Chapter XXXIX

We must therefore inquire what may be fittingly eaten or not by the rational and gentle [975] animal, which acts always in conformity with reason; and not worship at random, sheep, or goats, or kine; to abstain from which is an act of moderation, [976] for much advantage is derived by men from these animals. Whereas, is it not the most foolish of all things to spare crocodiles, and to treat *them* as sacred to some fabulous divinity or other? For it is a mark of exceeding stupidity to spare those animals which do not spare us, and to bestow care on those which make a prey of human beings. But Celsus approves of those who, in keeping with the laws of their country, worship and tend crocodiles, and not a word does he say against them, while the Christians appear deserving of censure, who have been taught to loath evil, and to turn away from wicked works, and to reverence and honour virtue as being generated by God, and as being His Son. For we must not, on account of their feminine name and nature, regard wisdom and righteousness as females; [977] for these things are in our view the Son of God, as His genuine disciple has shown, when he said of Him, "Who of God is made to us wisdom, and righteousness, and sanctification, and redemption." [978] And although we may call Him a "second" God, let men know that by the term "second God" we mean nothing else than a virtue capable of including all other virtues, and a reason capable of containing all reason whatsoever which exists in all things, which have arisen naturally, directly, and for the general advantage, and which "reason," we say, dwelt in the soul of Jesus, and was united to Him in a degree far above all other souls, seeing He alone was enabled completely to receive the highest share in the absolute reason, and the absolute wisdom, and the absolute righteousness.

Chapter XL

But since, after Celsus had spoken to the above effect of the different kinds of laws, he adds the following remark, "Pindar appears to me to be correct in saying that law is king of all things," let us proceed to discuss this assertion. What law do you mean to say, good sir, is "king of all things?" If you mean those which exist in the various cities, then such an assertion is not true. For all men are not governed by the same law. You ought to have said that "laws are kings of all men," for in every nation some law is king of all. But if you mean that which is law in the proper sense, then it is this which is by nature "king of all things;" although there are some individuals who, having like robbers abandoned the law, deny its validity, and live lives of violence and injustice. We Christians, then, who have come to the knowledge of the law which is by nature "king of all things," and which is the same with the law of God, endeavour to regulate our lives by its prescriptions, having bidden a long farewell to those of an unholy kind.

Chapter XLI

Let us notice the charges which are next advanced by Celsus, in which there is exceedingly little that has reference to the Christians, as most of them refer to the Jews. His words are: "If, then, in these respects the Jews were carefully to preserve their own law, they are not to be blamed for so doing, but those persons rather who have forsaken their own usages, and adopted those of the Jews. And if they pride themselves on it, as being possessed of superior wisdom, and keep aloof from intercourse with others, as not being equally pure with themselves, they have already heard that their doctrine concerning heaven is not peculiar to them, but, to pass by all others, is one which has long ago been received by the Persians, as Herodotus somewhere mentions. 'For they have a custom,' he says, 'of going up to the tops of the mountains, and of offering sacrifices to Jupiter, giving the name of Jupiter to the whole circle of the heavens.' [979] And I think," continues Celsus, "that it makes no difference whether you call the highest being Zeus, or Zen, or Adonai, or Sabaoth, or Ammoun like the Egyptians, or Pappæus like the Scythians. Nor would they be deemed at all holier than others in this respect, that they observe the rite of circumcision, for this was done by the Egyptians and Colchians before them; nor because they abstain from swine's flesh, for the Egyptians practised abstinence not only from it, but from the flesh of goats, and sheep, and oxen, and fishes as well; while Pythagoras and his disciples do not eat beans, nor anything that contains life. It is not probable, however, that they enjoy God's favour, or are loved by Him differently from others, or that angels were sent from heaven to them alone, as if they had had allotted to them 'some region of the blessed,' [980] for we see both themselves and the country of which they were deemed worthy. Let this band, [981] then, take its departure, after paying the penalty of its vaunting, not having a knowledge of the great God, but being led away and deceived by the artifices of Moses, having become his pupil to no good end."

Chapter XLII

It is evident that, by the preceding remarks, Celsus charges the Jews with falsely giving themselves out as the chosen portion of the Supreme God above all other nations. And he accuses them of boasting, because they gave out that they knew the great God, although they did not really know Him, but were led away by the artifices of Moses, and were deceived by him, and became his disciples to no good end. Now we have in the preceding pages already spoken in part of the venerable and distinguished polity of the Jews, when it existed amongst them as a symbol of the city of God, and of His temple, and of the sacrificial worship offered in it and at the altar of sacrifice. But if any one were to turn his attention to the meaning of the legislator, and to the constitution which he established, and were to examine the various points relating to him, and compare them with the present method of worship among other nations, there are none which he would admire to a greater degree; because, so far as can be accomplished among mortals, everything that was not of advantage to the human race was withheld from them, and only those things which are useful bestowed. And for this reason they had neither gymnastic contests, nor scenic representations, nor horse-races; nor were there among them women who sold their beauty to any one who wished to have sexual intercourse without offspring, and to cast contempt upon the nature of human generation. And what an advantage was it to be taught from their tender years to ascend above all visible nature, and to hold the belief that God was not fixed anywhere within its limits, but to look for Him on high, and beyond the sphere of all bodily substance! [982] And how great was the advantage which they enjoyed in being instructed almost from their birth, and as soon as they could speak, [983] in the immortality of the soul, and in the existence of courts of justice under the earth, and in the rewards provided for those who have lived righteous lives! These truths, indeed, were proclaimed in the veil of fable to children, and to those whose views of things were childish; while to those who were already occupied in investigating the truth, and desirous of making progress therein, these fables, so to speak, were transfigured into the truths which were concealed within them. And I consider that it was in a manner worthy of their name as the "portion of God" that they despised all kinds of divination, as that which bewitches men to no purpose, and which proceeds rather from wicked demons than from anything of a better nature; and sought the knowledge of future events in the souls of those who, owing to their high degree of purity, received the spirit of the Supreme God.

Chapter XLIII

But what need is there to point out how agreeable to sound reason, and unattended with injury either to master or slave, was the law that one of the same faith [984] should not be allowed to continue in slavery more than six years? [985] The Jews, then, cannot be said to preserve their own law in the same points with the other nations. For it would be censurable in them, and would involve a charge of insensibility to the superiority of their law, if they were to believe that they had been legislated for in the same way as the other nations among the heathen. And although Celsus will not admit it, the Jews nevertheless *are* possessed of a wisdom superior not only to that of the multitude, but also of those who have the appearance of philosophers; because those who engage in philosophical pursuits, after the utterance of the most venerable philosophical sentiments, fall away into the worship of idols and demons, whereas the very lowest Jew directs his look to the Supreme God alone; and they do well, indeed, so far as this point is concerned, to pride themselves thereon, and to keep aloof from the society of others as accursed and impious. And would that they had not sinned, and transgressed the law, and slain the prophets in former times, and in these latter days conspired against Jesus, that we might be in possession of a pattern of a heavenly city which even Plato would have sought to describe; although I doubt whether he could have accomplished as much as was done by Moses and those who followed him, who nourished a "chosen generation," and "a holy nation," dedicated to God, with words free from all superstition.

Chapter XLIV

But as Celsus would compare the venerable customs of the Jews with the laws of certain nations, let us proceed to look at them. He is of opinion, accordingly, that there is no difference between the doctrine regarding "heaven" and that regarding "God;" and he says that "the Persians, like the Jews, offer sacrifices to Jupiter upon the tops of the mountains,"—not observing that, as the Jews were acquainted with one God, so they had only one holy house of prayer, and one altar of whole burnt-offerings, and one censer for incense, and one high priest of God. The Jews, then, had nothing in common with the Persians, who ascend the summits of their mountains, which are many in number, and offer up sacrifices which have nothing in common with those which are regulated by the Mosaic code,— in conformity to which the Jewish priests "served unto the example and shadow of heavenly things," explaining enigmatically the object of the law regarding the sacrifices, and the things of which these sacrifices were the symbols. The Persians therefore may call the "whole circle of heaven" Jupiter; but we maintain that "the heaven" is neither Jupiter nor God, as we indeed know that certain beings of a class inferior to God have ascended above the heavens and all visible nature: and in this sense we understand the words, "Praise God, ye heaven of heavens, and ye waters that be above the heavens; let them praise the name of the Lord." [986]

Chapter XLV

As Celsus, however, is of opinion that it matters nothing whether the highest being be called Jupiter, or Zen, or Adonai, or Sabaoth, or Ammoun (as the Egyptians term him), or Pappæus (as the Scythians entitle him), let us discuss the point for a little, reminding the reader at the same time of what has been said above upon this question, when the language of Celsus led us to consider the subject. And now we maintain that the nature of names is not, as Aristotle supposes, an enactment of those who impose them. [987] For the languages which are prevalent among men do not derive their origin from men, as is evident to those who are able to ascertain the nature of the charms which are appropriated by the inventors of the languages differently, according to the various tongues, and to the varying pronunciations of the names, on which we have spoken briefly in the preceding pages, remarking that when those names which in a certain language were possessed of a natural power were translated into another, they were no longer able to accomplish what they did before when uttered in their native tongues. And the same peculiarity is found to apply to men; for if we were to translate the name of one who was called from his birth by a certain appellation in the Greek language into the Egyptian or Roman, or any other tongue, we could not make him do or suffer the same things which he would have done or suffered under the appellation first bestowed upon him. Nay, even if we translated into the Greek language the name of an individual who had been originally invoked in the Roman tongue, we could not produce the result which the incantation professed itself capable of accomplishing had it preserved the name first conferred upon him. And if these statements are true when spoken of the names of *men*, what are we to think of those which are transferred, for any cause whatever, to the *Deity*? For example, something is transferred [988] from the name Abraham when translated into Greek, and something is signified by that of Isaac, and also by that of Jacob; and accordingly, if any one, either in an invocation or in swearing an oath, were to use the expression, "the God of Abraham," and "the God of Isaac," and "the God of Jacob," he would produce certain effects, either owing to the nature of these names or to their powers, since even demons are vanquished and become submissive to him who pronounces these names; whereas if we say, "the god of the chosen father of the echo, and the god of laughter, and the god of him who strikes with the heel," [989] the mention of the name is attended with no result, as is the case with other names possessed of no power. And in the same way, if we translate the word "Israel" into Greek or any other language, we shall produce no result; but if we retain it as it is, and join it to those expressions to which such as are skilled in these matters think it ought to be united, there would then follow some result from the pronunciation of the word which would accord with the professions of those who employ such invocations. And we may say the same also of the pronunciation of "Sabaoth," a word which is frequently employed in incantations; for if we translate the term into "Lord of hosts," or "Lord of armies," or "Almighty" (different acceptations of it having been proposed by the interpreters), we shall accomplish nothing; whereas if we retain the original pronunciation, we shall, as those who are skilled in such matters maintain, produce some effect. And the same observation holds good of Adonai. If, then, neither "Sabaoth" nor "Adonai," when rendered into what appears to be their meaning in the Greek tongue, can accomplish anything, how much less would be the result among those who regard it as a matter of indifference whether the highest being be called Jupiter, or Zen, or Adonai, or Sabaoth!

Chapter XLVI

It was for these and similar mysterious reasons, with which Moses and the prophets were acquainted, that they forbade the name of other gods to be pronounced by him who bethought himself of praying to the one Supreme God alone, or to be remembered by a heart which had been taught to be pure from all foolish thoughts and words. And for these reasons we should prefer to endure all manner of suffering rather than acknowledge Jupiter to be God. For we do not consider Jupiter and Sabaoth to be the same, nor Jupiter to be at all divine, but that some demon, unfriendly to men and to the true God, rejoices under this title. [990] And although the Egyptians were to hold Ammon before us under threat of death, we would rather die than address him as God, it being a name used in all probability in certain Egyptian incantations in which this demon is invoked. And although the Scythians may call Pappæus the supreme God, yet we will not yield our assent to this; granting, indeed, that there *is* a Supreme Deity, although we do not give the name Pappæus to Him as His proper title, but regard it as one which is agreeable to the demon to whom was allotted the desert of Scythia, with its people and its language. He, however, who gives God His title in the Scythian tongue, or in the Egyptian or in any language in which he has been brought up, will not be guilty of sin.

Chapter XLVII

Now the reason why circumcision is practised among the Jews is not the same as that which explains its existence among the Egyptians and Colchians, and therefore it is not to be considered the same circumcision. And as he who sacrifices does not sacrifice to the same god, although he appears to perform the rite of sacrifice in a similar manner, and he who offers up prayer does not pray to the same divinity, although he asks the same things in his supplication; so, in the same way, if one performs the rite of circumcision, it by no means follows that it is not a different act from the circumcision performed upon another. For the purpose, and the law, and the wish of him who performs the rite, place the act in a different category. But that the whole subject may be still better understood, we have to remark that the term for "righteousness" [991] is the same among all the Greeks; but righteousness is shown to be one thing according to the view of Epicurus; and another according to the Stoics, who deny the threefold division of the soul; and a different thing again according to the followers of Plato, who hold that righteousness is the proper business of the parts of the soul. [992] And so also the "courage" [993] of Epicurus is one thing, who would undergo some labours in order to escape from a greater number; and a different thing that of the philosopher of the Porch, who would choose all virtue for its own sake; and a different thing still that of Plato, who maintains that virtue itself is the act of the irascible part of the soul, and who assigns to it a place about the breast. [994] And so circumcision will be a different thing according to the varying opinions of those who undergo it. But on such a subject it is unnecessary to speak on this occasion in a treatise like the present; for whoever desires to see what led us to the subject, can read what we have said upon it in the Epistle of Paul to the Romans.

Chapter XLVIII

Although the Jews, then, pride themselves on circumcision, they will separate it not only from that of the Colchians and Egyptians, but also from that of the Arabian Ishmaelites; and yet the latter was derived from their ancestor Abraham, the father of Ishmael, who underwent the rite of circumcision along with his father. The Jews say that the circumcision performed on the eighth day is the principal circumcision, and that which is performed according to circumstances is different; and probably it was performed on account of the hostility of some angel towards the Jewish nation, who had the power to injure such of them as were not circumcised, but was powerless against those who had undergone the rite. This may be said to appear from what is written in the book of Exodus, where the angel before the circumcision of Eliezer [995] was able to work against [996] Moses, but could do nothing after his son was circumcised. And when Zipporah had learned this, she took a pebble and circumcised her child, and is recorded, according to the reading of the common copies, to have said, "The blood of my child's circumcision is stayed," but according to the Hebrew text, "A bloody husband art thou to me." [997] For she had known the story about a certain angel having power before the shedding of the blood, but who became powerless through the blood of circumcision. For which reason the words were addressed to Moses, "A bloody husband art thou to me." But these things, which appear rather of a curious nature, and not level to the comprehension of the multitude, I have ventured to treat at such length; and now I shall only add, as becomes a Christian, one thing more, and shall then pass on to what follows. For this angel might have had power, I think, over those of the people who were not circumcised, and generally over all who worshipped only the Creator; and this power lasted so long as Jesus had not assumed a human body. But when He had done this, and had undergone the rite of circumcision in His own person, all the power of the angel over those who practise the same worship, but are not circumcised, [998] was abolished; for Jesus reduced it to nought by [the power of] His unspeakable divinity. And therefore His disciples are forbidden to circumcise themselves, and are reminded [by the apostle]: "If ye be circumcised, Christ shall profit you nothing." [999]

Chapter XLIX

But neither do the Jews pride themselves upon abstaining from swine's flesh, as if it were some great thing; but upon their having ascertained the nature of clean and unclean animals, and the cause of the distinction, and of swine being classed among the unclean. And these distinctions were signs of certain things until the advent of Jesus; after whose coming it was said to His disciple, who did not yet comprehend the doctrine concerning these matters, but who said, "Nothing that is common or unclean hath entered into my mouth," [1000] "What God hath cleansed, call not thou common." It therefore in no way affects either the Jews or us that the Egyptian priests abstain not only from the flesh of swine, but also from that of goats, and sheep, and oxen, and fish. But since it is not that "which entereth into the mouth that defiles a man," and since "meat does not commend us to God," we do not set great store on refraining from eating, nor yet are we induced to eat from a gluttonous appetite. And therefore, so far as we are concerned, the followers of Pythagoras, who abstain from all things that contain life, may do as they please; only observe the different reason for abstaining from things that have life on the part of the Pythagoreans and our ascetics. For the former abstain on account of the fable about the transmigration of souls, as the poet says:

"And some one, lifting up his beloved son,
Will slay him after prayer; O how foolish he!" [1001]

We, however, when we do abstain, do so because "we keep under our body, and bring it into subjection," [1002] and desire "to mortify our members that are upon the earth, fornication, uncleanness, inordinate affection, evil concupiscence;" [1003] and we use every effort to "mortify the deeds of the flesh." [1004]

Chapter L

Celsus, still expressing his opinion regarding the Jews, says: "It is not probable that they are in great favour with God, or are regarded by Him with more affection than others, or that angels are sent by Him to them alone, as if to them had been allotted some region of the blessed. For we may see both the people themselves, and the country of which they were deemed worthy." We shall refute this, by remarking that it is evident that this nation *was* in great favour with God, from the fact that the God who presides over all things was called the God of the Hebrews, even by those who were aliens to our faith. And because they were in favour with God, they were not abandoned by Him; [1005] but although few in number, they continued to enjoy the protection of the divine power, so that in the reign of Alexander of Macedon they sustained no injury from him, although they refused, on account of certain covenants and oaths, to take up arms against Darius. They say that on that occasion the Jewish high priest, clothed in his sacred robe, received obeisance from Alexander, who declared that he had beheld an individual arrayed in this fashion, who announced to him in his sleep that he was to be the subjugator of the whole of Asia. Accordingly, we Christians maintain that "it was the fortune of that people in a remarkable degree to enjoy God's favour, and to be loved by Him in a way different from others;" but that this economy of things and this divine favour were transferred to us, after Jesus had conveyed the power which had been manifested among the Jews to those who had become converts to Him from among the heathen. And for this reason, although the Romans desired to perpetrate many atrocities against the Christians, in order to ensure their extermination, they were unsuccessful; for there was a divine hand which fought on their behalf, and whose desire it was that the word of God should spread from one corner of the land of Judea throughout the whole human race.

Chapter LI

But seeing that we have answered to the best of our ability the charges brought by Celsus against the Jews and their doctrine, let us proceed to consider what follows, and to prove that it is no empty boast on our part when we make a profession of knowing the great God, and that we have not been led away by any juggling tricks [1006] of Moses (as Celsus imagines), or even of our own Saviour Jesus; but that for a good end we listen to the God who speaks in Moses, and have accepted Jesus, whom he testifies to be God, as the Son of God, in hope of receiving the best rewards if we regulate our lives according to His word. And we shall willingly pass over what we have already stated by way of anticipation on the points, "whence we came, and who is our leader, and what law proceeded from Him." And if Celsus would maintain that there is no difference between us and the Egyptians, who worship the goat, or the ram, or the crocodile, or the ox, or the river-horse, or the dog-faced baboon, [1007] or the cat, he can ascertain if it be so, and so may any other who thinks alike on the subject. We, however, have to the best of our ability defended ourselves at great length in the preceding pages on the subject of the honour which we render to our Jesus, pointing out that we have found the better part; [1008] and that in showing that the truth which is contained in the teaching of Jesus Christ is pure and unmixed with error, we are not commending ourselves, but our Teacher, to whom testimony was borne through many witnesses by the Supreme God and the prophetic writings among the Jews, and by the very clearness of the case itself, for it is demonstrated that He could not have accomplished such mighty works without the divine help.

Chapter LII

But the statement of Celsus which we wish to examine at present is the following: "Let us then pass over the refutations which might be adduced against the claims of their teacher, and let him be regarded as really an angel. But is he the first and only one who came [to men], or were there others before him? If they should say that he is the only one, they would be convicted of telling lies against themselves. For they assert that on many occasions others came, and sixty or seventy of them together, and that these became wicked, and were cast under the earth and punished with chains, and that from this source originate the warm springs, which are their tears; and, moreover, that there came an angel to the tomb of this said being—according to some, indeed, one, but according to others, two—who answered the women that he had arisen. For the Son of God could not himself, as it seems, open the tomb, but needed the help of another to roll away the stone. And again, on account of the pregnancy of Mary, there came an angel to the carpenter, and once more another angel, in order that they might take up the young child and flee away [into Egypt]. But what need is there to particularize everything, or to count up the number of angels said to have been sent to Moses, and others amongst them? If, then, others were sent, it is manifest that he also came from the same God. But he may be supposed to have the appearance of announcing something of greater importance [than those who preceded him], as if the Jews had been committing sin, or corrupting their religion, or doing deeds of impiety; for these things are obscurely hinted at."

Chapter LIII

The preceding remarks might suffice as an answer to the charges of Celsus, so far as regards those points in which our Saviour Jesus Christ is made the subject of special investigation. But that we may avoid the appearance of intentionally passing over any portion of his work, as if we were unable to meet him, let us, even at the risk of being tautological (since we are challenged to this by Celsus), endeavour as far as we can with all due brevity to continue our discourse, since perhaps something either more precise or more novel may occur to us upon the several topics. He says, indeed, that "he has omitted the refutations which have been adduced against the claims which Christians advance on behalf of their teacher," although he has *not* omitted anything which he was able to bring forward, as is manifest from his previous language, but makes this statement only as an empty rhetorical device. That we are not refuted, however, on the subject of our great Saviour, although the accuser may *appear* to refute us, will be manifest to those who peruse in a spirit of truth-loving investigation all that is predicted and recorded of Him. And, in the next place, since he considers that he makes a concession in saying of the Saviour, "Let him appear to be really an angel," we reply that we do not accept of such a concession from Celsus; but we look to the work of Him who came to visit the whole human race in His word and teaching, as each one of His adherents was capable of receiving Him. And this was the work of one who, as the prophecy regarding Him said, was not simply an angel, but the "Angel of the great council:" [1009] for He announced to men the great counsel of the God and Father of all things regarding them, [saying] of those who yield themselves up to a life of pure religion, that they ascend by means of their great deeds to God; but of those who do not adhere to Him, that they place themselves at a distance from God, and journey on to destruction through their unbelief of Him. He then continues: "If even the angel came to men, is he the first and only one who came, or did others come on former occasions?" And he thinks he can meet either of these dilemmas at great length, although there is not a single real Christian who asserts that Christ was the only being that visited the human race. For, as Celsus says, "If they should say the only one," there are others who appeared to different individuals.

Chapter LIV

In the next place, he proceeds to answer himself as he thinks fit in the following terms: "And so he is not the only one who is recorded to have visited the human race, as even those who, under pretext of teaching in the name of Jesus, have apostatized from the Creator as an inferior being, and have given in their adherence to one who is a superior God and father of him who visited [the world], assert that before him certain beings came from the Creator to visit the human race." Now, as it is in the spirit of truth that we investigate all that relates to the subject, we shall remark that it is asserted by Apelles, the celebrated disciple of Marcion, who became the founder of a certain sect, and who treated the writings of the Jews as fabulous, that Jesus is the only one that came to visit the human race. Even against him, then, who maintained that Jesus was the only one that came from God to men, it would be in vain for Celsus to quote the statements regarding the descent of other angels, seeing Apelles discredits, as we have already mentioned, the miraculous narratives of the Jewish Scriptures; and much more will he decline to admit what Celsus has adduced, from not understanding the contents of the book of Enoch. No one, then, convicts us of falsehood, or of making contradictory assertions, as if we maintained both that our Saviour was the only being that ever came to men, and yet that many others came on different occasions. And in a most confused manner, moreover, does he adduce, when examining the subject of the visits of angels to men, what he has derived, without seeing its meaning, from the contents of the book of Enoch; for he does not appear to have read the passages in question, nor to have been aware that the books which bear the name of Enoch do not at all circulate in the churches as divine, although it is from this source that he might be supposed to have obtained the statement, that "sixty or seventy angels descended at the same time, who fell into a state of wickedness."

Chapter LV

But, that we may grant to him in a spirit of candour what he has not discovered in the contents of the book of Genesis, that "the sons of God, seeing the daughters of men, that they were fair, took to them wives of all whom they chose," we shall nevertheless even on this point persuade those who are capable of understanding the meaning of the prophet, that even before us there was one who referred this narrative to the doctrine regarding souls, which became possessed with a desire for the corporeal life of men, and this in metaphorical language, he said, was termed "daughters of men." But whatever may be the meaning of the "sons of God desiring to possess the daughters of men," it will not at all contribute to prove that Jesus was not the only one who visited mankind as an angel, and who manifestly became the Saviour and benefactor of all those who depart from the flood of wickedness. Then, mixing up and confusing whatever he had at any time heard, or had anywhere found written—whether held to be of divine origin among Christians or not—he adds: "The sixty or seventy who descended together were cast under the earth, and were punished with chains." And he quotes (as from the book of Enoch, but without naming it) the following: "And hence it is that the tears of these angels are warm springs,"—a thing neither mentioned nor heard of in the churches of God! For no one was ever so foolish as to materialize into human tears those which were shed by the angels who had come down from heaven. And if it were right to pass a jest upon what is advanced against us in a serious spirit by Celsus, we might observe that no one would ever have said that hot springs, the greater part of which are fresh water, were the tears of the angels, since tears are saltish in their nature, unless indeed the angels, in the opinion of Celsus, shed tears which are fresh.

Chapter LVI

Proceeding immediately after to mix up and compare with one another things that are dissimilar, and incapable of being united, he subjoins to his statement regarding the sixty or seventy angels who came down from heaven, and who, according to him, shed fountains of warm water for tears, the following: "It is related also that there came to the tomb of Jesus himself, according to some, two angels, according to others, one;" having failed to notice, I think, that Matthew and Mark speak of one, and Luke and John of two, which statements are not contradictory. For they who mention "one," say that it was he who rolled away the stone from the sepulchre; while they who mention "two," refer to those who appeared in shining raiment to the women that repaired to the sepulchre, or who were seen within sitting in white garments. Each of these occurrences might now be demonstrated to have actually taken place, and to be indicative of a figurative meaning existing in these "phenomena," [and intelligible] to those who were prepared to behold the resurrection of the Word. Such a task, however, does not belong to our present purpose, but rather to an exposition of the gospel.

Chapter LVII

Now, that miraculous appearances have sometimes been witnessed by human beings, is related by the Greeks; and not only by those of them who might be suspected of composing fabulous narratives, but also by those who have given every evidence of being genuine philosophers, and of having related with perfect truth what had happened to them. Accounts of this kind we have read in the writings of Chrysippus of Soli, and also some things of the same kind relating to Pythagoras; as well as in some of the more recent writers who lived a very short time ago, as in the treatise of Plutarch of Chæronea "on the Soul," and in the second book of the work of Numenius the Pythagorean on the "Incorruptibility of the Soul." Now, when such accounts are related by the Greeks, and especially by the philosophers among them, they are not to be received with mockery and ridicule, nor to be regarded as fictions and fables; but when those who are devoted to the God of all things, and who endure all kinds of injury, even to death itself, rather than allow a falsehood to escape their lips regarding God, announce the appearances of angels which they have themselves witnessed, they are to be deemed unworthy of belief, and their words are not to be regarded as true! Now it is opposed to sound reason to judge in this way whether individuals are speaking truth or falsehood. For those who act honestly, only after a long and careful examination into the details of a subject, slowly and cautiously express their opinion of the veracity or falsehood of this or that person with regard to the marvels which they may relate; since it is the case that neither do all men show themselves worthy of belief, nor do all make it distinctly evident that they are relating to men only fictions and fables. Moreover, regarding the resurrection of Jesus from the dead, we have this remark to make, that it is not at all wonderful if, on such an occasion, either one or two angels should have appeared to announce that Jesus had risen from the dead, and to provide for the safety of those who believed in such an event to the advantage of their souls. Nor does it appear to me at all unreasonable, that those who believe in the resurrection of Jesus, and who manifest, as a fruit of their faith not to be lightly esteemed, their possession of a virtuous [1010] life, and their withdrawal from the flood of evils, should not be unattended by angels who lend their help in accomplishing their conversion to God.

Chapter LVIII

But Celsus challenges the account also that an angel rolled away the stone from the sepulchre where the body of Jesus lay, acting like a lad at school, who should bring a charge against any one by help of a string of commonplaces. And, as if he had discovered some clever objection to the narrative, he remarks: "The Son of God, then, it appears, could not open his tomb, but required the aid of another to roll away the stone." Now, not to overdo the discussion of this matter, or to have the appearance of unreasonably introducing philosophical remarks, by explaining the figurative meaning at present, I shall simply say of the narrative alone, that it does appear in itself a more respectful proceeding, that the servant and inferior should have rolled away the stone, than that such an act should have been performed by Him whose resurrection was to be for the advantage of mankind. I do not speak of the desire of those who conspired against the Word, and who wished to put Him to death, and to show to all men that He *was* dead and non-existent, [1011] that His tomb should not be opened, in order that no one might behold the Word alive after their conspiracy; but the "Angel of God" who came into the world for the salvation of men, with the help of another angel, proved more powerful than the conspirators, and rolled away the weighty stone, that those who deemed the Word to be dead might be convinced that He is not with the "departed," but is alive, and precedes those who are willing to follow Him, that He may manifest to them those truths which come after those which He formerly showed them at the time of their first entrance [into the school of Christianity], when they were as yet incapable of receiving deeper instruction. In the next place, I do not understand what advantage he thinks will accrue to his purpose when he ridicules the account of "the angel's visit to Joseph regarding the pregnancy of Mary;" and again, that of the angel to warn the parents "to take up the new-born child, whose life was in danger, and to flee with it into Egypt." Concerning these matters, however, we have in the preceding pages answered his statements. But what does Celsus mean by saying, that "according to the Scriptures, angels are recorded to have been sent to Moses, and others as well?" For it appears to me to contribute nothing to his purpose, and especially because none of them made any effort to accomplish, as far as in his power, the conversion of the human race from their sins. Let it be granted, however, that other angels were sent from God, but that he came to announce something of greater importance [than any others who preceded him]; and when the Jews had fallen into sin, and corrupted their religion, and had done unholy deeds, transferred the kingdom of God to other husbandmen, who in all the churches take special care of themselves, [1012] and use every endeavour by means of a holy life, and by a doctrine conformable thereto, to win over to the God of all things those who would rush away from the teaching of Jesus. [1013]

Chapter LIX

Celsus then continues: "The Jews accordingly, and these (clearly meaning the Christians), have the same God;" and as if advancing a proposition which would not be conceded, he proceeds to make the following assertion: "It is certain, indeed, that the members of the great church [1014] admit this, and adopt as true the accounts regarding the creation of the world which are current among the Jews, viz. concerning the six days and the seventh;" on which day, as the Scripture says, God "ceased" [1015] from His works, retiring into the contemplation of Himself, but on which, as Celsus says (who does not abide by the letter of the history, and who does not understand its meaning), God "rested," [1016] —a term which is not found in the record. With respect, however, to the creation of the world, and the "rest [1017] which is reserved after it for the people of God," the subject is extensive, and mystical, and profound, and difficult of explanation. In the next place, as it appears to me, from a desire to fill up his book, and to give it an appearance of importance, he recklessly adds certain statements, such as the following, relating to the first man, of whom he says: "We give the same account as do the Jews, and deduce the same genealogy from him as they do." However, as regards "the conspiracies of brothers against one another," we know of none such, save that Cain conspired against Abel, and Esau against Jacob; but not Abel against Cain, nor Jacob against Esau: for if this had been the case, Celsus would have been correct in saying that we give the same accounts as do the Jews of "the conspiracies of brothers against one another." Let it be granted, however, that we speak of the same descent into Egypt as they, and of their return [1018] thence, which was not a "flight," [1019] as Celsus considers it to have been, what does that avail towards founding an accusation against us or against the Jews? Here, indeed, he thought to cast ridicule upon us, when, in speaking of the Hebrew people, he termed their exodus a "flight;" but when it was his business to investigate the account of the punishments inflicted by God upon Egypt, that topic he purposely passed by in silence.

Chapter LX

If, however, it be necessary to express ourselves with precision in our answer to Celsus, who thinks that we hold the same opinions on the matters in question as do the Jews, we would say that we both agree that the books [of Scripture] were written by the Spirit of God, but that we do *not* agree about the meaning of their contents; for we do not regulate our lives like the Jews, because we are of opinion that the literal acceptation of the laws is not that which conveys the meaning of the legislation. And we maintain, that "when Moses is read, the veil is upon their heart," [1020] because the meaning of the law of Moses has been concealed from those who have not welcomed [1021] the way which is by Jesus Christ. But we know that if one turn to the Lord (for "the Lord is that Spirit"), the veil being taken away, "he beholds, as in a mirror with unveiled face, the glory of the Lord" in those thoughts which are concealed in their literal expression, and to his own glory becomes a participator of the divine glory; the term "face" being used figuratively for the "understanding," as one would call it without a figure, in which is the face of the "inner man," filled with light and glory, flowing from the true comprehension of the contents of the law.

Chapter LXI

After the above remarks he proceeds as follows: "Let no one suppose that I am ignorant that some of them will concede that their God is the same as that of the Jews, while others will maintain that he is a different one, to whom the latter is in opposition, and that it was from the former that the Son came." Now, if he imagine that the existence of numerous heresies among the Christians is a ground of accusation against Christianity, why, in a similar way, should it not be a ground of accusation against philosophy, that the various sects of philosophers differ from each other, not on small and indifferent points, but upon those of the highest importance? Nay, medicine also ought to be a subject of attack, on account of its many conflicting schools. Let it be admitted, then, that there are amongst us some who deny that our God is the same as that of the Jews: nevertheless, on that account those are not to be blamed who prove from the same Scriptures that one and the same Deity is the God of the Jews and of the Gentiles alike, as Paul, too, distinctly says, who was a convert from Judaism to Christianity, "I thank my God, whom I serve from my forefathers with a pure conscience." [1022] And let it be admitted also, that there is a third class who call certain persons "carnal," and others "spiritual" (I think he here means the followers of Valentinus): yet what does this avail against us, who belong to the church, and who make it an accusation against such as hold that certain natures are saved, and that others perish in consequence of their natural constitution? [1023] And let it be admitted further, that there are some who give themselves out as Gnostics, in the same way as those Epicureans who call themselves philosophers: yet neither will they who annihilate the doctrine of providence be deemed true philosophers, nor those true Christians who introduce monstrous inventions, which are disapproved of by those who are the disciples of Jesus. Let it be admitted, moreover, that there are some who accept Jesus, and who boast on that account of being Christians, and yet would regulate their lives, like the Jewish multitude, in accordance with the Jewish law,—and these are the twofold sect of Ebionites, who either acknowledge with us that Jesus was born of a virgin, or deny this, and maintain that He was begotten like other human beings,—what does that avail by way of charge against such as belong to the church, and whom Celsus has styled "those of the multitude?" [1024] He adds, also, that certain of the Christians are believers in the Sibyl, [1025] having probably misunderstood some who blamed such as believed in the existence of a prophetic Sibyl, and termed those who held this belief Sibyllists.

Chapter LXII

He next pours down upon us a heap of names, saying that he knows of the existence of certain Simonians who worship Helene, or Helenus, as their teacher, and are called Helenians. But it has escaped the notice of Celsus that the Simonians do not at all acknowledge Jesus to be the Son of God, but term Simon the "power" of God, regarding whom they relate certain marvellous stories, saying that he imagined that if he could become possessed of similar powers to those with which he believed Jesus to be endowed, he too would become as powerful among men as Jesus was amongst the multitude. But neither Celsus nor Simon could comprehend how Jesus, like a good husbandman of the word of God, was able to sow the greater part of Greece, and of barbarian lands, with His doctrine, and to fill these countries with words which transform the soul from all that is evil, and bring it back to the Creator of all things. Celsus knows, moreover, certain Marcellians, so called from Marcellina, and Harpocratians from Salome, and others who derive their name from Mariamne, and others again from Martha. We, however, who from a love of learning examine to the utmost of our ability not only the contents of Scripture, and the differences to which they give rise, but have also, from love to the truth, investigated as far as we could the opinions of philosophers, have never at any time met in with these sects. He makes mention also of the Marcionites, whose leader was Marcion.

Chapter LXIII

In the next place, that he may have the appearance of knowing still more than he has yet mentioned, he says, agreeably to his usual custom, that "there are others who have wickedly invented some being as their teacher and demon, and who wallow about in a great darkness, more unholy and accursed than that of the companions of the Egyptian Antinous." And he seems to me, indeed, in touching on these matters, to say with a certain degree of truth, that there are certain others who have wickedly invented another demon, and who have found him to be their lord, as they wallow about in the great darkness of their ignorance. With respect, however, to Antinous, who is compared with our Jesus, we shall not repeat what we have already said in the preceding pages. "Moreover," he continues, "these persons utter against one another dreadful blasphemies, saying all manner of things shameful to be spoken; nor will they yield in the slightest point for the sake of harmony, hating each other with a perfect hatred." Now, in answer to this, we have already said that in philosophy and medicine sects are to be found warring against sects. We, however, who are followers of the word of Jesus, and have exercised ourselves in thinking, and saying, and doing what is in harmony with His words, "when reviled, bless; being persecuted, we suffer it; being defamed, we entreat;" [1026] and we would *not* utter "all manner of things shameful to be spoken" against those who have adopted different opinions from ours, but, if possible, use every exertion to raise them to a better condition through adherence to the Creator alone, and lead them to perform every act as those who will [one day] be judged. And if those who hold different opinions will not be convinced, we observe the injunction laid down for the treatment of such: "A man that is a heretic, after the first and second admonition, reject, knowing that he that is such is subverted, and sinneth, being condemned of himself." [1027] Moreover, we who know the maxim, "Blessed are the peacemakers," and this also, "Blessed are the meek," would not regard with hatred the corrupters of Christianity, nor term those who had fallen into error Circes and flattering deceivers. [1028]

Chapter LXIV

Celsus appears to me to have misunderstood the statement of the apostle, which declares that "in the latter times some shall depart from the faith, giving heed to seducing spirits and doctrines of devils, speaking lies in hypocrisy, having their conscience seared with a hot iron, forbidding to marry, and commanding to abstain from meats, which God hath created to be received with thanksgiving of them who believe;" [1029] and to have misunderstood also those who employed these declarations of the apostle against such as had corrupted the doctrines of Christianity. And it is owing to this cause that Celsus has said that "certain among the Christians are called 'cauterized in the ears;'" [1030] and also that some are termed "enigmas," [1031] —a term which we have never met. The expression "stumbling-block" [1032] is, indeed, of frequent occurrence in these writings,—an appellation which we are accustomed to apply to those who turn away simple persons, and those who are easily deceived, from sound doctrine. But neither we, nor, I imagine, any other, whether Christian or heretic, know of any who are styled Sirens, who betray and deceive, [1033] and stop their ears, and change into swine those whom they delude. And yet this man, who affects to know everything, uses such language as the following: "You may hear," he says, "all those who differ so widely, and who assail each other in their disputes with the most shameless language, uttering the words, 'The world is crucified to me, and I unto the world.'" And this is the only phrase which, it appears, Celsus could remember out of Paul's writings; and yet why should we not also employ innumerable other quotations from the Scriptures, such as, "For though we do walk in the flesh, we do not war after the flesh; (for the weapons of our warfare are not carnal, but mighty through God to the pulling down of strongholds,) casting down imaginations, and every high thing that exalteth itself against the knowledge of God?" [1034]

Chapter LXV

But since he asserts that "you may hear all those who differ so widely saying, 'The world is crucified to me, and I unto the world,'" we shall show the falsity of such a statement. For there are certain heretical sects which do not receive the epistles of the Apostle Paul, as the two sects of Ebionites, and those who are termed Encratites. Those, then, who do not regard the apostle as a holy and wise man, will not adopt his language, and say, "The world is crucified to me, and I unto the world." And consequently in this point, too, Celsus is guilty of falsehood. He continues, moreover, to linger over the accusations which he brings against the diversity of sects which exist, but does not appear to me to be accurate in the language which he employs, nor to have carefully observed or understood how it is that those Christians who have made progress in their studies say that they are possessed of greater knowledge than the Jews; and also, whether they acknowledge the same Scriptures, but interpret them differently, or whether they do not recognise these books as divine. For we find both of these views prevailing among the sects. He then continues: "Although they have no foundation for their doctrine, let us examine the system itself; and, in the first place, let us mention the corruptions which they have made through ignorance and misunderstanding, when in the discussion of elementary principles they express their opinions in the most absurd manner on things which they do not understand, such as the following." And then, to certain expressions which are continually in the mouths of the believers in Christianity, he opposes certain others from the writings of the philosophers, with the object of making it appear that the noble sentiments which Celsus supposes to be used by Christians have been expressed in better and clearer language by the philosophers, in order that he might drag away to the study of philosophy those who are caught by opinions which at once evidence their noble and religious character. We shall, however, here terminate the fifth book, and begin the sixth with what follows.

Footnotes

842 . Cf. Prov. x. 19.

843 . Cf. 2 Tim. ii. 15.

844 . Cf. 2 Cor. x. 5.

845 . Cf. Ps. lxviii. 11.

846 . τοῖς ἐκεῖ θεοῖς.

847 . ἀψίδα.

848 . κατέρχεσθαι.

849 . Cf. Heb. i. 14.

850 . ἐν τοῖς καθαρωτάτοις τοῦ κόσμου χωρίοις ἐπουρανίοις, ἢ καὶ τοῖς τούτων καθαρωτέροις ὑπερουρανίοις.

851 . Cf. Ps. lxxxvi. 8, xcvi. 4, cxxxvi. 2.

852 . ἐὰν δυνώμεθα κατακούειν τῆς περὶ προσευχῆς κυριολεξίας καὶ καταχρήσεως.

853 . ἢ τοὺς μὲν ἐν σκότῳ ποῦ ἐκ γοητείας οὐκ ὀρθῆς τυφλώττουσιν, ἢ δι᾽ ἀμυδρῶν φασμάτων ὀνειρώττουσιν ἐγχρίμπτειν λεγομένους, εὖ μάλα θρησκεύειν.

854 . Cf. Ex. xx. 3, 4, 5.

855 . Cf. Deut. iv. 19.

856 . τὸ ὅλον ὁ κόσμος.

857 . Cf. Jer. vii. 17, 18.

858 . Cf. Acts vii. 42, 43.

859 . Cf. Col. ii. 18, 19.

860 . ἐγγαστριμύθοις.

861 . ἐπαοιδοῖς.

862 . Cf. Lev. xix. 31.

863 . The emendations of Ruæus have been adopted in the translation, the text being probably corrupt. Cf. Ruæus, *in loc.*

864 . Cf. Deut. iv. 19, 20.

865 . Cf. 1 Pet. ii. 9.

866 . Cf. Gen. xv. 5.

867 . Cf. Deut. i. 10.

868 . χώματι.

869 . ἀπὸ τῶν δικαίων τῶν πολλῶν.

870 . Cf. Dan. xii. 1, 2, 3.

871 . Cf. 1 Cor. xv. 40-42.

872 . μεγαλοφυῶς.

873 . Matt. v. 14.

874 . Cf. Matt. v. 16.

875 . Cf. Origen, *de Principiis*, i. c. vii.

876 . ἐκ τοῦ ἐν αὐτοῖς αὐτεξουσίου ἐληλυθός.

877 . Cf. 1 John i. 5.

878 . μύδρον διάπυρον.

879 . τὴν εὐκτικὴν δύναμιν.

880 . Cf. Matt. xix. 17; cf. Mark x. 18.

881 . Ibid.

882 . Cf. Deut. vi. 13.

883 . Cf. Ps. cvii. 20.

884 . προνοητικῶς.

885 . Matt. xxviii. 20.

886 . Cf. John i. 26, 27.

887 . Cf. Jer. xxiii. 24.

888 . Cf. Jer. xxiii. 23.

889 . ζητεῖν εὔχεσθαι τῷ μὴ φθάνοντι ἐπὶ τὰ σύμπαντα.

890 . Cf. Rom. viii. 19-21.

891 . Cf. Ps. cxlviii. 3.

892 . Cf. Rom. viii. 19-21.

893 . ὥσπερ μάγειρος.

894 . οὐ γὰρ τῆς πλημμελοῦς ὀρέξεως, οὐδὲ τῆς πεπλανημένης ἀκοσμίας, ἀλλὰ τῆς ὀρθῆς καὶ δικαίας φύσεως Θεός ἐστιν ἀρχηγέτης.

895 . ὕλην.

896 . Cf. 1 Cor. iii. 12.

897 . Cf. Mal. iii. 2.

898 . Cf. Ezek. xxii. 18, 20.

899 . πόνου καὶ πυρός.

900 . Cf. Isa. xlvii. 14, 15.

901 . τὰ σκυθρωπά.

902 . Cf. Isa. xlviii. 9 (Septuagint).

903 . Cf. 1 Cor. i. 21.

904 . τὰ κατὰ τοὺς τόπους.

905 . Cf. John v. 39.

906 . καὶ τῶν πολλῶν κακῶν ἀποχήν.

907 . Cf. 1 Cor. xv. 51, 52.

908 . Cf. 1 Thess. iv. 15, 16.

909 . Cf. 1 Thess. iv. 16, 17.

910 . περὶ τοῦ προβλήματος τούτου.

911 . Cf. Eph. iv. 14.

912 . Cf. 1 Cor. xv. 35-38.

913 . ἐν ἐλαίας πυρῆνι.

914 . Cf. 1 Cor. xv. 42, 43.

915 . Cf. 1 Cor. xv. 48, 49.

916 . Cf. 1 Cor. xv. 49.

917 . Cf. 1 Cor. xv. 50.

918 . Cf. Tobit xii. 7.

919 . διὰ τὰς τοπικὰς μεταβάσεις.

920 . Cf. Ps. xxxvii. 30.

921 . σφόδρ' ἀπεμφαίνοντα.

922 . μυχθίζειν.

923 . κατὰ τὸ ἐνδεχόμενον.

924 . καὶ τὴν τοῦ ἐφ' ἡμῖν φύσιν γιγνώσκοντες ἐνδεχομένον ἃ ἐνδέχεται.

925 . βούλημα.

926 . Cf. Matt. xxiv. 35; cf. Mark xiii. 31.

927 . λόγος.

928 . διαλεκτικαῖς ἀνάγκαις.

929 . εἰ δὲ χρὴ βεβιασμένως ὀνομάσαι.

930 . βδελυρόν.

931 . Cf. John i. 1.

932 . καὶ κατὰ τὸ ἐπιχώριον νόμους θέμενοι.

933 . τὰ μέρη τῆς γῆς ἐξ ἀρχῆς ἄλλα ἄλλοις ἐπόπταις νενεμημένα.

934 . καὶ κατά τινας ἐπικρατείας διειλημμένα.

935 . παραλύειν.

936 . καταθοινᾶται.

937 . σωφροσύνη.

938 . ἐφάπτεται.

939 . οἰκειοτέρους.

940 . Cf. Deut. xxxii. 8, 9 (LXX.).

941 . Cf. Gen. xi. 1, 2.

942 . σύγχυσις.

943 . Cf. Gen. xi. 5-9.

944 . Cf. Wisd. of Sol. x. 5.

945 . Cf. Tobit xii. 7.

946 . Cf. Wisd. of Sol. i. 4.

947 . ἐς ὅσον εἰσὶ τὰ τοῦ φωτὸς καὶ τοῦ ἀπὸ φωτὸς ἀϊδίου ἀπαυγάσματος φρονοῦντες.

948 . ἀλλότρια ἀνατολῶν φρονοῦντες.

949 . τὰ τῆς ὕλης.

950 . πολιτείᾳ.

951 . καὶ τίσαντας δίκην.

952 . ὡσπερεὶ παιδευθέντας.

953 . ἀπὸ τῆς πάντων μερίδος.

954 . Cf. Rom. i. 24, 26, 28.

955 . ἀλλὰ καὶ βουλόμεθα, οὐχ ὅπη ἦ ἐκείνοις φίλον, ποιεῖν τὰ ἐκείνων.

956 . Ps. ii. 8.

957 . χοροστάτην.

958 . Cf. 1 Tim. iii. 15.

959 . Cf. Isa. ii. 3.

960 . ἐλένχῃ.

961 . ἀρχηγέτην.

962 . συγκόψαι τὰς πολεμικὰς ἡμῶν λογικὰς μαχαίρας καὶ ὑβριστικὰς εἰς ἄροτρα, καὶ τὰς κατὰ τὸ πρότερον ἡμῶν μάχιμον ζιβύνας εἰς δρέπανα μετασκευάζομεν.

963 . Cf. Isa. ii. 4.

964 . Cf. Jer. xvi. 19 and xiv. 22: ὡς ψευδῆ ἐκτήσαντο οἱ πατέρες ἡμῶν εἴδωλα, καὶ οὐκ ἔστιν ἐν αὐτοῖς ὑετίζων.

965 . Cf. Herodot. ii. 18.

966 . ὁ δὲ Ἄμμων οὐδέν τι κακίων διαπρεσβεῦσαι τὰ δαιμόνια, ἢ οἱ Ἰουδαίων ἄγγελοι.

967 . εὐφημεῖν μὲν ἐκέλευον.

968 . Cf. Herodot. iii. 38.

969 . γέλοιος ἂν εἴη φιλόσοφος ἀφιλόσοφα πράττων.

970 . φυσιολογίαν.

971 . πρεσβύτατον πάντων τῶν δημιουργημάτων.

972 . Cf. Gen. i. 26.

973 . This sentence is regarded by Guietus as an interpolation, which should be struck out of the text.

974 . ἵνα δόξῃ μετὰ τῶν ἀτελέστων τελετῶν, καὶ τῶν καλουσῶν δαίμονας μαγγανειῶν, οὐχ ὑπὸ ἀγαλματοποιῶν μόνων κατασκευάζεσθαι θεός, ἀλλὰ καὶ ὑπὸ μάγων, καὶ φαρμακῶν, καὶ τῶν ἐπῳδαῖς αὐτῶν κηλουμένων δαιμόνων.

975 . ἡμέρῳ.

976 . μέτριον.

977 . οὐ γὰρ παρὰ τὸ θηλυκὸν ὄνομα, καὶ τῇ οὐσίᾳ θήλειαν νομιστέον εἶναι τὴν σοφίαν, καὶ τὴν δικαιοσύνην.

978 . Cf. 1 Cor. i. 30.

979 . Cf. Herodot. i. 135.

980 . οἷον δή τινα μακάρων χώραν λαχοῦσιν.

981 . χορός.

982 . ὑπὲρ τὰ σώματα.

983 . συμπληρώσει τοῦ λόγου.

984 . τὸν ἀπὸ τῶν αὐτῶν ὁρώμενον δογμάτων.

985 . Cf. Ex. xxi. 2 and Jer. xxxiv. 14.

986 . Cf. Ps. cxlviii. 4, 5.

987 . ὅτι ἡ τῶν ὀνομάτων φύσις οὐ θεμένων εἰσὶ νόμοι.

988 . μεταλαμβάνεται γάρ τι, φερ' εἰπεῖν. In the editions of Hœschel and Spencer, τι is wanting.

989 . ὁ θεὸς πατρὸς ἐκλεκτοῦ τῆς ἠχοῦς, καὶ ὁ θεὸς τοῦ γέλωτος, καὶ ὁ θεὸς τοῦ πτερνιστοῦ. Cf. note in Benedictine ed.

990 . δαίμονα δέ τινα χαίρειν οὕτως ὀνομαζόμενον.

991 . δικαιοσύνη.

992 . ἰδιοπραγίαν τῶν μερῶν τῆς ψυχῆς.

993 . ἀνδρεία.

994 . τοῦ θυμικοῦ μέρους τῆς ψυχῆς φάσκοντος αὐτὸ εἶναι ἀρετὴν, καὶ ἀποτάσσοντος αὐτῇ τόπον τὸν περὶ τὸν θωράκα.

995 . Cf. Ex. iv. 24, 25. Eliezer was one of the two sons of Moses. Cf. Ex. xviii. 4.

996 . ἐνεργεῖν κατὰ Μωϋσέως.

997 . Cf. Ex. iv. 25, 26.

998 . κατὰ τῶν ἐν τῇ θεοσεβείᾳ ταύτῃ περιτεμνομένων δύναμις. Boherellus inserts μὴ before περιτεμνομένων, which has been adopted in the text.

999 . Gal. v. 2.

1000 . Cf. Acts x. 14.

1001 . A quotation:

καί τις φίλον υἱὸν ἀείρας,

σφάξει ἐπευχόμενος μέγα νήπιος.

—A verse of Empedocles, quoted by Plutarch, *de Superstitione*, c. xii. Spencer. Cf. note *in loc.* in Benedictine edition.

1002 . Cf. 1 Cor. ix. 27.

1003 . Cf. Col. iii. 5.

1004 . Cf. Rom. viii. 13.

1005 . καὶ ὡς εὐδοκιμοῦντες γε ὅσον οὐκ ἐγκατελείποντο. The negative particle (οὐκ) is wanting in the editions of Hœschel and Spencer, but is found in the Royal, Basil, and Vatican MSS. Guietus would delete ὅσον (which emendation has been adopted in the translation), while Boherellus would read ὅσοι instead.—Ruæus.

1006 . γοητείᾳ.

1007 . τὸν κυνοκέφαλον.

1008 . ὅτι κρεῖττον εὕρομεν.

1009 . Cf. Isa. ix. 6.

1010 . τὸν ἐῤῥωμένον βίον.

1011 . καὶ τὸ μηδὲν τυγχάνοντα.

1012 . ἑαυτῶν. Guietus would read αὐτῶν, to agree with τῶν ἐκκλησιῶν.

1013 . Instead of τὰς ἀπὸ τῆς διδασκαλίας τοῦ Ἰησοῦ ἀφορμάς, Boherellus conjectures τοὺς ... ἀφορμῶντας, which has been adopted in the translation.

1014 . τῶν ἀπὸ μεγάλης ἐκκλησίας.

1015 . κατέπαυσεν.

1016 . ἀναπαυσάμενος.

1017 . σαββατισμοῦ.

1018 . τὴν ἐκεῖθεν ἐπάνοδον.

1019 . φυγὴν.

1020 . 2 Cor. iii. 15.

1021 . ἀσπασαμένοις.

1022 . 2 Tim. i. 3.

1023 . ἐκ κατασκευῆς.

1024 . ἀπὸ τοῦ πλήθους.

1025 . Σιβυλλιστάς.

1026 . 1 Cor. iv. 12, 13.

1027 . Tit. iii. 10.

1028 . Κίρκας καὶ κύκηθρα αἱμύλα.

1029 . Cf. 1 Tim. iv. 1-3.

1030 . ἀκοῆς καυστήρια. Cf. note in Benedictine ed.

1031 . αἰνίγματα. Cf. note in Benedictine ed.

1032 . σκανδάλου.

1033 . ἐξορχουμένας καὶ σοφιστρίας.

1034 . Cf. 2 Cor. x. 3.